# 100
# Mindfulness
# Meditations

## Neil Seligman

CONSCIOUS
HOUSE

**CONSCIOUS
HOUSE**

First published in 2016 by Conscious House

ISBN 978-0-9955232-0-3

Conscious House is a trading name of The Conscious Professional Limited
UK Company Registration Number: 08128111

**Cover Design**
Jack Newman

**Interior Layout Design**
Silke Spingies

**Cover Photograph**
Soul Portrait of Arian Levanael by Neil Seligman

Visit **www.conscioushouse.org** for author interviews
and to sign up for information on new releases
by Neil Seligman and other authors.

For Flynn and Piper.


With deep thanks to:


Mum and Dad whose love welcomed me into this World.

To Adrian and Chess who showed the way.

To Jack, whose love I cherish dearly.

To Ty, who teaches me the art of play.

To JJ, Paul, Stephen, David and my teacher Georgina,

you were the champions of my creative heart, before I knew how.


*And not forgetting Robert Watson in Australia*
*whose kindness and wisdom has made writing this book a joyful delight.*

What you seek, is seeking you.

RUMI

## Mindfulness Is ...

An experience for you to discover.

Within these pages, you will find 100 invitations into the rich realm of your own awareness. What you learn within, will be your personal wisdom. What you find, will be yourself.

Why believe in anyone else's version of mindfulness when mindfulness lives inside of you and is ready in every moment to reveal itself in the presence of your listening.

## My Mindfulness

On my 7th birthday I took to the new piano as if I had been playing it all my life. As my fingers stumbled over the keys I felt connected to a deep intelligence beyond my years. This was my first experience of mindfulness.

It sounded terrible but I persevered, imagining what it must feel like to rouse the instrument like a master.

It was in those moments that I touched in for the first time with a pure experience of creative energy. It felt amazing and I would return to the piano several times a day to play my feelings. Sometimes I would look at an artwork on the wall and 'play the painting' pretending to be the tumultuous ocean, the sun setting over the hills or the lonesome horse and hounds.

I now know, those were my first meditations.

To this day I still sit down regularly to play my feelings, touch in with the energy of creativity and see what music is moving through me.

I no longer need the piano.

This is my mindfulness.

# Contents

# How To Use This Book

At various times, readers might consider themselves beginners, capable, seasoned, or even lapsed mindfulness enthusiasts. The journey of mindfulness is rarely a straight line so wherever you are right now, I suggest reading through all of the following section before you set off into the practices.

## Progression through the practices

Beginners should work through Part A thoroughly first to ensure comfort with the foundational meditations before moving on to more involved practices. Practices 1, 2 and 3 are essential pre-reading for all of the other practices. After familiarising yourself with those, there is no need to work through the rest of Part A in order (although that would work too). Feel free to pick and choose based on your personal circumstances and what you are drawn to each day.

Over time, you will find your favourites for repeated practice.

Part B is designed to offer more specific practices that help you integrate mindfulness skills in daily life. Choose relevant practices that relate to your current situation, or simply allow your curiosity to guide you.

You will find some of the practices more challenging than others so listen to your intuition and gauge whether today is the right time to approach a difficult topic. There is a rhythm to everything in life, including your readiness for self-exploration and increased mindfulness. Take your time and follow along gently, as your practice unfolds. If difficulties prevail, consider seeking the guidance and support of a friend, mindfulness teacher or healthcare professional.

Before delving into the Advanced Practices of Part C, make sure you feel stable, confident and comfortable in the space of your inner silence.

All of the practices are designed to last between five and fifteen minutes so, depending on how much time you have available, set a timer for five, ten or fifteen minutes.

If you particularly like a practice and would like to follow it as an audio, you might record yourself with your phone, tablet or computer. Simply read through the script, adding to it as you wish, and allowing appropriate silent space.

Additionally there is an audio album to accompany this book titled: *10 Mindfulness Meditations*.

## For more experienced meditators

For solo mindfulness explorers and connoisseurs you might flick through the book and chance upon the next exercise to deepen your practice.

However, start with Practices 1, 2 and 3 as they lay the foundations for the rest of the book and will familiarise you with its format and style. After that, journey forward and inward as you wish, picking and choosing the ones that have most appeal on any given day.

Remember that the 'beginner' practices can often be the most revealing, particularly when you are able to return to them with fresh and abundant curiosity each time.

## For families, couples, friends and small groups practising together

If you are practising together you can take turns reading the instructions adding flourishes and details to make them your own. Where it feels right, repeat instructions and add silent space to allow the listeners to have their own internal experience. Look over the Guidance For Leading Others in Practice for more on this.

For families: This book can sit on the bedside table ready for tonight's mindfulness practice before bed, or on the kitchen table for a mindfulness activity before school.

For couples: Take turns guiding each other on your mindfulness journeys each morning or evening. After practice, spend some time discussing your discoveries and experience.　　　　　　**»**

For friends: Have fun playing some of the mindfulness games and activities in your free time, sharing practices when you get together and discussing your discoveries over dinner.

For small groups: This book can be pulled out at your gatherings to inspire shared practice and discussion afterwards.

## Your mindfulness journal

Journaling enriches the learning process by creating a reason to reflect and as such is a wonderful way to embed new discoveries and deepen your mindfulness practice.

A diary is a record of events in your life: *Went to Niagara Falls and the noise was deafening.* A journal is a consciously written reflection: *The power of water to carve through layers of rock makes me wonder about how many insurmountable problems might be solved using methods which at first glance seem wholly inappropriate.*

Sometimes, you will feel like there is very little progress being made. Looking back over your Mindfulness Journal entries will show you just how far you have come, and in time, your notes will become a valuable record of the ups and downs of your life.

At the end of most practices will be a reminder to record your experience in your Mindfulness Journal, so if you do not already have one, I recommend buying a notebook to serve that purpose. Find one with a cover that inspires you and with blank, not lined, inside pages. The blank pages will challenge you to be creative as you journal, so if you feel the urge to draw something alongside your notes, absolutely do so. Allow the doodles to mix with the words.

Enjoy the time dedicated to reflecting on your inner journeys, and let journaling become an integral part of your mindfulness practice.

## For mindfulness teachers

As a mindfulness teacher, you know that preparing original meditations for class can be a lengthy process, so this book will be a useful resource that saves you time.

You will be able to draw teaching points from the quotation, Invitation and Mindful Tip. Add to these your own teachings and stories.

Feel free to adapt the practices to suit your own needs.

## Guidance for leading others in practice

If you strike a tuning fork it will hum. If you bring another one close to it, it will also start to sing. Mindfulness practice is similar. If you are leading the practice, you are the first tuning fork. It is your job to lead the way, not just when you are speaking, but when you are quiet too.

So as you read the instructions, set an intention to be clear, audible and present, and follow them fully yourself.

In the silences, breathe deeply and settle into your own experience.

If you do so, you cannot go wrong.

Now breathe ... and if you are ready, enter.

Part A

# FOUNDATIONS FOR MINDFULNESS PRACTICE

# Posture, Breathing and Attitude

# 1 Basic Posture

## Sometimes, simply by sitting, the soul collects wisdom.

ZEN PROVERB

## Invitation

The first three practices are essential foundations. It is important to know how to sit and how to find the way into and out of inner awareness. The journey begins by considering posture.

The spine is the Antenna of Awareness. Holding it tall and alert will allow your awareness to be clear and strong. If the spine is slumping or slouching, awareness will be distracted and weak. Try it for yourself and see.

For each practice, choose whether to sit on a chair, on the floor, or to lie down. All have benefits and will teach you something new about the relationship between your unique body, your mind and awareness. Experiment with postures and find the ones that work for you.

Remember also that the way you enter your posture will become part of your ritual of meditation, so be aware as you walk to your seat, take care as you arrange your body, and notice what feelings arise as you approach each day's practice.

## Mindful Tip

With all this focus on posture, do not forget that if you were floating inside the International Space Station in zero gravity, meditation would still be possible! In fact, mindful awareness is always possible, in any position, at any time.

# PRACTICE 1

## VARIATION 1 - Sitting on a chair

1. Choose a chair with a comfortable seat and sit down normally.

2. Now, notice the body. Take a little inventory. Have you slumped backwards? Is your back curved or straight? Are your shoulders forward, central or back?

3. Place your middle fingertip at the base of the spine (the sacrum). Place your other middle finger on the crown of your head. Imagine there is a little piece of string connecting the sacrum to the crown.

4. Breathe.

5. Next, imagine pulling up on the string. Allow the imagined movement of the string to bring alignment to the spine. Notice how the spine responds by becoming taller, straighter and more dynamic.

6. If your body has not already naturally moved away from the back of the chair, allow this to occur so your back is now fully self-supporting.

7. Then, allow the head to drop forward by a centimetre, no more.

8. Your lips should be touching, your teeth slightly apart.

9. Imagine that your spine is the Antenna of Awareness.

## VARIATION 2 - Sitting cross-legged on the floor

1. For most, sitting cross-legged on the floor without support is uncomfortable. However, this can easily be remedied by sitting on one or more meditation/yoga blocks whilst resting your ankles on a cushion. Take as many blocks as you need. Some people use four or five.

2. Continue from Step 2 in Variation 1 above.

## VARIATION 3 - Kneeling

1. Kneeling can be made comfortable by straddling two or more meditation/yoga blocks placed lengthways between the legs. This will raise the body up and let the legs fold naturally behind you.

2. Continue from Step 2 in Variation 1 above.

## VARIATION 4 - Lying down

1. Set up a yoga mat in a quiet room, perhaps one with plenty of light streaming in. As most people associate lying down with sleeping, this posture is not appropriate when very tired or at bedtime.

2. Consider carefully whether a pillow is needed, as these are generally associated with sleep. You may find a perfectly comfortable position without one and be less prone to drift off into a snooze!  »

3. Lie down and allow the legs to rotate outwards naturally. The hands and arms can fall at each side with palms turned upwards.

4. Adjust the body until it feels straight, spacious and comfortable. Check that the head, spine and lower body are aligned and straight.

# 2 Awareness of Breathing

Breathing in, I calm body and mind.
Breathing out, I smile.
Dwelling in the present moment
I know this is the only moment.

THICH NHAT HANH

## Invitation

In many of the wisdom traditions, the breath holds huge significance as the doorway to awareness.

As you build your mindfulness practice day by day, begin by feeling the specific sensations of breathing and learn to follow the journey taken by the breath in and out of the body.

The Variations described in this exercise can be followed as stand-alone practices or used as an entry into others.

## Mindful Tip

When people are stressed their breath becomes shallow and tight.

If this happens to you ask: *Where is my breath?*

Pay close attention to your chest, airways and lungs. Notice if there is a constriction, in which case choose consciously to breathe deeply.

Allow the inhale to bring awareness to the body and the exhale to release tension.

With practice, a natural breathing rhythm will quickly return.

»

# PRACTICE 2

Begin by settling into your posture. Allow the gaze to soften and the eyes to close.

## VARIATION 1 - Following the breath

1. Inhale and exhale naturally through your nose.

2. Bring your full attention to the sensations of the breath. There is no need to change it in any way.

3. Feel the air moving through your nostrils as it begins its journey into the body.

4. Can you sense the movement of air, a change in temperature, an increase in pressure?

5. Next, the breath travels up into the nose before changing direction and moving down the airways into the lungs. Can you feel exactly where the air changes direction? Take five breaths here focusing on the physical sensations found at that point.

6. As the air moves down into the body, experience the lungs expanding, filling and then releasing.

7. On each subsequent complete breath, travel all the way in and all the way out. Inhale. Exhale.

8. Repeat as desired attending fully to the smallest sensations.

## VARIATION 2 - The four phases of breath

1. Inhale and exhale naturally through your nose.

2. Bring your full attention to the sensations of the breath allowing it to be exactly as it is. There is no need to change it in any way.

3. Imagine the breath is a wave moving through your body.

4. The breath has four phases that make up its rhythm:

   *Inhalation*
   *Pause*
   *Exhalation*
   *Pause*

5. Focus on each of the four in turn noticing how they differ.

6. As you continue attending to the four phases of the breath, notice how each whole breath is slightly different from the one before.

7. Follow the unique rhythm of each breath.

8. Repeat as desired attending fully to the smallest sensations.

## VARIATION 3 – Counting the breath

1. Inhale and exhale naturally through your nose.

2. Bring your full attention to the physical sensations of the breath.

3. Feel the air moving through your nostrils as the air begins its journey into the body.

4. As you inhale, silently count *one*; as you exhale, repeat *one*. Then, inhale *two*, exhale *two* and so on up to *ten*, then start again.

5. Choose 5, 10 or as many cycles as you wish.

6. Then let go of the counts but allow your focus to stay with the movement of breath in the body.

7. Notice the quality of your breathing right now.

8. Is your breathing slower than at the beginning of the exercise? Is it deeper? How calm do you feel now?

# 3 Return to Wakefulness

## Do not cry because it's over, smile because it happened.

DR SEUSS

### Invitation

As each practice comes to a close, there is much to be grateful for. Time has been dedicated to pure reflection, to gentle noticing and conscious being. There is no need to cling to what is now passed. The gifts of your practice are there to take into each new day.

### Mindful Tip

Experiment with the Variations that follow and find your favourites.

# PRACTICE 3

At the end of most practices that follow in this book is an invitation to return to wakefulness. Here are some suggestions to help you do just that.

## VARIATION 1 - Following the breath

1. Bring your awareness once again to the physical sensations of the breath. Feel the rhythm of this exchange that underlies each and every moment.

2. Notice the four phases of the breath. Inhale. Pause. Exhale. Pause.

3. Feel how your breathing has changed since the beginning of this practice.

4. Silently choose three words to describe the breath.

5. Feel the rise and fall of the chest. Notice the sensation of clothing on skin.

6. Remember the flow of air passing through the nose. Feel each individual sensation.

7. In your very own time, allow the eyes to open and take a few breaths to fully transition into eyes-open wakefulness.

## VARIATION 2 - Staged return: self / mind / body / breath

1. On your next inhale, sit with the question: *What does it feel like to be me in this moment?* Take five breaths here, and listen.

2. Now bring your attention to mind. Without judgment, silently choose three words that describe your current state of mind. Take five breaths here.

3. Next, bring your awareness to the body. Notice the effect of gravity on your feet, seat and hands. Focus on the simple sensations that remind you of your physical being. Participate in these sensations; really allow yourself to be your experience. Take five breaths here.

4. Finally, return to the simplicity of inhale and exhale, to the flow of life that travels on the air. Notice how body and breath are connected: intertwined: inseparable.

5. Take five conscious breaths and gradually return to wakefulness.

»

## VARIATION 3 - Gathering wisdom

1. Having been on an inner journey, now it is time to reflect.

2. What have you experienced? Take five breaths in contemplation.

3. What challenges have you faced? Take five breaths in contemplation.

4. What have you learned? Take five breaths in contemplation.

5. What wisdom have you found? Take five breaths in contemplation.

6. In your very own time, allow the eyes to open and take a few breaths to fully transition into eyes-open wakefulness.

## VARIATION 4 - Visualising the room before opening the eyes

1. In letting go of this practice, become fully aware of the breath and the body.

2. Notice the weight of the body, its temperature and the unique rhythm of each inhalation and exhalation.

3. Now, with your eyes still closed, recall what is in the room. Imagine seeing through the eyelids.

4. Visualise the space carefully. Be specific and detailed. Take five breaths here.

5. When completely ready, allow the eyes to open and notice the degree of accuracy in your visualisation.

## VARIATION 5 - Silence

On some days, nothing more is needed other than silence to carry you home.

1. Sit within the silence of your practice until ready to open your eyes. You will know the right moment when you feel an internal sense of completion.

## VARIATION 6 - Transition into sleep

This Variation works best when read by another, or listened to on a recording.

1. Let the focus of your mindfulness practice fade into the background. The time for work is done.

2. Allow the wisdom of your day to settle into your heart and breathe deeply into peacefulness, relaxation and calm. There is nothing to cling to. There is nothing to do.

3. Settle down into bed, gather the covers and sink a little deeper into the mattress. Find a position of total relaxation. That's right. Perfect.

4. Surrounded by love, release the mind into abstract associations, reverie and dreams. Reverie and dreams. Dreams.

5. You have everything you need. The time for work is done.

6. The breath goes on and on and enters every cell, completing unfinished thoughts, resolving tension and sweeping mind and body clean.

7. Peacefulness gathers in your heart.

8. Tranquillity cascades through the warmth of your body.

9. Awareness drifts, the body rests, the breath goes on and on and on.

10. Surrounded by love, the dreamer dreams.

11. The joyful heart sleeps away.

12. Surrounded by love, the dreamer dreams.

13. The joyful heart sleeps away.

Congratulations.

You have now completed the essential pre-reading. Venture onwards in the order of your choice and at your own pace.

# 4 Belly Breathing

## Breath is the link between mind and body.

DAN BRULE

## Invitation

The breath is a reminder that there is an exchange going on inside each of us in every moment of the day. Much more than the passage of oxygen and carbon dioxide, life itself is on its journey through you.

In each moment, the breath is a beautiful and effortless collaboration with the Universe.

## Mindful Tip

This practice develops the capacity of self-compassion.

When connecting with the body, do so with a loving touch and an intention to bring calm, as if comforting a baby, or stroking a beloved pet.

Bringing this depth of compassionate awareness to self can be challenging, so gradually open to it in your own time. Do not worry if it feels awkward or uncomfortable at first. Stay with it.

By returning to the practice on subsequent days, the discomfort will ease and the practice will flow more naturally.

# PRACTICE 4

In this practice massage the belly and focus on what happens to the breath, the body and awareness. The exercise works just as well lying down, or seated, so experiment and see which works best. You may find that lying down and going through this practice before sleep allows you to relax and drift off with ease.

Begin by finding a comfortable posture and by bringing your attention to the breath. Take a few moments to let yourself arrive and allow the breath to draw you gently into internal awareness. Allow the gaze to soften, the eyes to close.

1. Bring the attention to the belly and notice how it is moving with each inhalation and exhalation. Take five breaths here.

2. Now place one hand on the skin so the belly button is beneath the centre of your palm.

3. Gently and slowly massage the belly by moving the palm in an increasing clockwise circle towards your hips and then in a decreasing clockwise circle back to the belly button. The hand remains in contact with the body throughout.

4. Once returned to the belly button, start the cycle again and repeat five times.

5. Now allow the hand to come to rest and take five breaths here.

6. How has your breathing responded? Is it slower, deeper, more peaceful?

7. On your next breath, without forcing it, pull the breath into the belly. Allow in as much air as feels comfortable. Take five breaths in this way: full inhale: full exhale.

8. Pause for a few moments by returning to a natural breathing rhythm.

9. Then, repeat the five belly breaths twice more, each time pausing afterwards to notice what has occurred.

10. Return to wakefulness in your own way.

Record your experience in your Mindfulness Journal noting the specific responses of the body and the breath.

If practising with others, take turns sharing your discoveries.

# 5 Heartfulness

Your task is not to seek for love,
but merely to seek and find all the
barriers within yourself that you have
built against it.

RUMI

## Invitation

The word for mindfulness and heartfulness in many Asian languages is the same word. When practising mindfulness people are also aiming to practise heartfulness. The idea of heart-centred awareness is therefore central to the practice.

## Mindful Tip

To know heart is to hear and experience the presence of wisdom within the body. Within the soft space of inner silence, heart whispers truth.

Be patient with your heart. You cannot ask a flower to open by shouting at it. You can only wait.

# PRACTICE 5

Begin by finding a comfortable posture and by bringing your attention to the breath. Take a few moments to let yourself arrive and allow the breath to draw you gently into internal awareness. Allow the gaze to soften, the eyes to close.

1. Inhale and visualise the breath being drawn directly into the heart. As you exhale see the breath moving back out into the space around you. As you do so, let the breath draw awareness into the heart-space.

2. Observe any sensations, images, feelings and thoughts that arise. Take five breaths here.

3. As awareness grows in the heart, notice how this feels and silently choose three words to describe this experience.

4. As you inhabit the heart fully and listening deepens, imagine what wisdom is available here. Silently say: *I ask for the teachings of heart.*

5. Listen and be present to whatever comes.

6. Now focus on a loving relationship in your life and allow the feelings of love to fill your heart. Notice the vibration of love itself. Feel it. Embrace it. Enrich it. Be with it fully. Take five breaths here.

7. Notice the feelings of gratitude and appreciation that arise as you contemplate the love already present in your life. Take five breaths here.

8. Allow the heart to show you the love that you already are. Take five breaths here.

9. Return to wakefulness in your own way.

Record your experience in your Mindfulness Journal noting the sensations, images, feelings and thoughts that arose from your heart. At your first attempt, you may only record one or two things, however keep revisiting this Practice because your awareness will develop.

If practising with others, take turns sharing your discoveries.

# 6 Mindfulness of Sounds

## Let go of your mind and then be mindful. Close your ears and listen!

RUMI

## Invitation

In my morning meditation I am sometimes joined by Ty (a large labrador) who tries all his tricks to get my attention.

I close my eyes, he nuzzles my ears. I centre myself, he licks my face. I focus on my breath, he rams a toy in my hand. I ignore him, he sits squarely on my lap.

Now sometimes I acquiesce and we play together on the floor. In those moments I try to be fully present with him and the game becomes something of a meditation itself.

Other times, he gives up his nuzzling and sits quietly at my side. We then both journey inward, he to sleep, and me into meditation.

Ty has taught me that an authentic mindfulness practice cannot be overly rigid and must include space for the spontaneous and the unexpected.

## Mindful Tip

In this practice, listen to the sounds around you and pay vivid attention, as if you were hearing birdsong for the very first time.

# PRACTICE 6

Begin by finding a comfortable posture and by bringing your attention to the breath. Take a few moments to let yourself arrive and allow the breath to draw you gently into internal awareness. Allow the gaze to soften, the eyes to close.

1. Wait.

2. Listen.

3. What can you hear?

4. Silently name three specific sounds: e.g.

   *The hum of electrical equipment*
   *The sounds of traffic*
   *Distant birdsong*

5. Now bring your focus to a single sound. Pay full attention to it. Describe it silently to yourself using five single words. If listening to the ocean your words might be:

   *Wave, Crash, Smooth, Wash, Sweep.*

6. Take five breaths here and fully explore the sound.

7. If the mind wanders, gently bring it back to the sound by finding something new about it. Take five further breaths here as you listen closely.

8. Next, repeat instructions 5–7 for your second and third sounds.

9. Return to wakefulness in your own way.

Record your experience and your chosen sounds and words in your Mindfulness Journal.

If practising with others, take turns sharing your discoveries.

# 7 Musical Mindfulness

## If music be the food of love, play on.

WILLIAM SHAKESPEARE

## Invitation

In the early stages of learning mindfulness meditation, one of the most important moments comes when realising that the attention has wandered. This realisation of distraction allows for a return of awareness to the focus of your practice. It is very important to know that this realisation does not signify failure and need not be met with judgment or despair. On the contrary, it shows that both focus and awareness are growing.

In this practice the focus will be on a piece of music of your choice.

## Mindful Tip

In this exercise, the length of your chosen music will determine the length of the practice. Mix things up by picking something unfamiliar or, if you do pick an old favourite, try to listen as if hearing it for the first time.

# PRACTICE 7

Choose a piece of music and press play.

Begin by finding a comfortable posture and by bringing your attention to the breath. Take a few moments to let yourself arrive and allow the breath to draw you gently into internal awareness. Allow the gaze to soften, the eyes to close.

1. Imagine you composed this music; that it flowed into the World directly from your heart.

2. Listen with clarity and allow yourself to be drawn into the melody, the rhythm, the movement and the emotion.

3. Feel the vibration of the music in every cell of your body.

4. What emotions arise? Pay full attention to any feelings present and notice their subtle movement through the body.

5. If the mind wanders from the focus of the music, bring it back patiently and compassionately.

6. Continue connecting and reconnecting with the piece.

7. Imagine that the music is flowing out of you now.

8. What do you see? What do you feel? What do you sense?

9. Take five breaths here.

10. Breathe and follow the music until it ends.

11. Return to wakefulness in your own way.

Record your experience of what you saw, felt and sensed in your Mindfulness Journal.

If practising with others, take turns sharing your discoveries.

# 8 Presence

**Be happy in the moment; that's enough. Each moment is all we need, not more.**

MOTHER TERESA

## Invitation

Increased presence is one of the most wonderful gifts of mindfulness practice.

It is that feeling of spontaneous aliveness and alertness when fully available, in the present moment, to receive what life is serving up.

Take yourself back to the last time you arrived in an unknown or exotic place. The sounds, the smells, the colours all compete for attention as you try to take it all in. The experience is physical, visceral, vital and totally captivating.

This is presence.

## Mindful Tip

This is a very useful introductory practice that can be done with any number of people without thinking about posture or even closing the eyes.

# PRACTICE 8

There are three stages to this practice. Follow along and notice the impact of the instructions upon awareness.

## Notice

1. Become aware of your surroundings. Look around. Really drink in the scene. Silently name some of the things that are obvious and visible. Be specific and pay attention to details that might otherwise be glossed over. Take your time as you scan and notice.

## Meet

2. Notice yourself in the picture. Consider that there is a meeting occurring in this moment between you (the subject) and your surroundings (the object). See if you can hold the acknowledgement of both yourself and your surroundings simultaneously.

## Appreciate

3. There is always something to appreciate in every moment, even if only the next breath of life.

4. Reflect upon the uniqueness of this moment:

   *Perhaps this is the first time trying this exercise, the first time purposefully deciding to welcome increased presence.*

5. Without looking too far, it will be possible to find something unique and special within every moment of every day.

## Optional continuation

6. As you become more present, see how long the focus can be sustained. Notice more and more of your surroundings, meet them and find something to appreciate.

7. Take five breaths here.

8. Finally, notice how you feel.

9. What, if anything, has changed in your awareness since the exercise began.

Record your experience in your Mindfulness Journal noting in particular which part of the practice you found most rewarding.

If practising with others, take turns sharing your discoveries.

# The Body

# 9 Focusing on Simple Sensations

And to the open-handed the search for one who shall receive is joy greater than giving.

KAHLIL GIBRAN

## Invitation

Simple physical sensations provide a perfect subject for mindfulness contemplation.

Remember the feeling of running a hand along the railings of the park as a child? The jangling sounds, the rhythm of fingers jumping from rail to rail, the pressure, heat and texture. Carefree moments such as this may seem far away but can be reconnected with at any time, such as now in this practice.

## Mindful Tip

Remember, there are no success measures to any of these practices. Through mindfulness, you are increasing your resourcefulness as a human being, simply by showing up to practise. Let go of the need to judge, or score each practice, and welcome the experience of each new moment. In doing so, a world of new discoveries can open.

# PRACTICE 9

Begin by finding a comfortable posture and by bringing your attention to the breath. Take a few moments to let yourself arrive and allow the breath to draw you gently into internal awareness.

1. Choose a finger and run it very slowly down the palm of your other hand. Watch closely. Notice if there is a connection between what you are seeing and what you are feeling. Pay attention to both the finger and the palm.

2. Repeat the motion five times, each time a little slower.

3. Now, allow the gaze to soften, the eyes to close.

4. Run a finger down your palm again five times, even slower each time. Focus only on the physical sensations of the finger on the skin of the palm. What are these microscopic physical sensations saying about the texture and structure of your hand?

5. Now, silently choose five words that describe this experience of touch.

6. Take five breaths here.

7. Reflect on these questions:

   *What is touch?*
   *What happens during physical contact?*

8. Take five breaths here.

9. Return to wakefulness in your own way.

Record your experience in your Mindfulness Journal noting as many sensations and feelings as you can remember. If, during the practice, you noticed something new about the sense of touch, try to describe it as clearly as you can.

If practising with others, take turns sharing your discoveries.

# 10 Body Scan

Mindfulness means non-judgmental awareness. A direct knowing of what is going on inside and outside ourselves, moment by moment.

MARK WILLIAMS

## Invitation

The purpose of the body scan is to pay attention to what the body is feeling. By becoming attuned to the physical sensations that arise in each moment inside the body, mindful awareness is grounded and increased.

In today's busy world, people are more aware of their mind than their body. As a result, it is easy to miss subtle signals broadcast by the body, such as pain, hunger and thirst as they get crowded out by more distracting and pressing thoughts such as scheduling, to-do lists and worries.

In this exercise pay full attention to the body and allow your curiosity to lead you into a deeper relationship with what you find.

## Mindful Tip

The body scan can be practised in any posture. Experiment with different ones and see what suits you best.

If it is difficult to follow the exercise by tracing your attention through the body, it can help to add in a tense-and-release of the muscles in each body part. For example, beginning with the feet, start by clenching the feet and curling your toes for two seconds and then letting them go. Do the same with the calf muscles and so on as you continue the journey through the body. In this way, the physical sensations of holding on and letting go can guide you through the practice and give a sense of something tangible to notice as you go.

# PRACTICE 10

Begin by finding a comfortable posture and by bringing your attention to the breath. Take a few moments to let yourself arrive and allow the breath to draw you gently into internal awareness. Allow the gaze to soften, the eyes to close.

1. Breathe and notice the body. Remember it. Discover yourself in this moment as a physical being with weight, temperature, texture, colour and energy. Take five breaths here.

2. Are certain parts of your body calling for attention? An itch, a scratch? A shift of body weight? Attend to the body's needs until it is quietly resting at peace.

3. Now bring awareness to the feet and toes. What do you sense? What is present? What do your feet want you to know about how they are feeling in this moment? Take at least five breaths here and gather information.

4. On the next breath, allow your awareness to move up into the legs. How do they feel? Are they comfortable? Go slowly. Check in with the calves, shins, knees and thighs. Feel for temperature, movement and weight. Notice where you are holding on. Take at least five breaths here until ready to move on.

5. Bring your awareness now to the central core of the body: the abdomen and chest. Check in. Listen. Feel. *Be* in your body. Notice all sensations, images, feelings and words that arise and take five breaths here.

6. Next, bring your attention to the arms and hands. Let your awareness travel down through the upper limbs and into the fingers. Take your time and feel all of the sensations present. Simply notice. Whatever is there, whether it feels pleasant or challenging, take an inventory. Do not add any judgment or commentary to the sensation. Follow and breathe. Listen for five more breaths.

7. Finally awareness moves up through the neck and into the head. Breathe. Listen. Gather. Observe. Witness. Take at least five breaths here.

8. On the next breath set an intention to inhabit the body fully. Imagine the mind and body are one. Take five breaths here.

9. Return to wakefulness in your own way.

Draw the basic outline of your body in your Mindfulness Journal and then use shading, lines and comments to record your experience.

If practising with others, take turns sharing your discoveries.

# 11 Letting Go

In the end, just three things matter: how well we have lived; how well we have loved; how well we have learned to let go.

JACK KORNFIELD

## Invitation

What if your only job in this lifetime was to find all the knots in your body, the tangles in your mind and the fear in your heart and dissolve them? Where would you start? How would you begin?

Individuals are here to discover how to open, how to love and how to live in compassionate awareness with, and of, one another.

In order to bring forth this compassion, it is necessary to let go of the tightness and constraint held within the body.

## Mindful Tip

This is a wonderful practice if you need to relax and let the day fall away. It will help you come back to your senses and find the clearing in your awareness where calmness resides.

## PRACTICE 11

Begin by finding a comfortable posture and by bringing your attention to the breath. Take a few moments to let yourself arrive and allow the breath to draw you gently into internal awareness. Allow the gaze to soften, the eyes to close.

1. Bring awareness to the mind and offer it an invitation: *Let go.* Repeat the words *Let go* five times and allow your mind to release, expand, ease and relax. Take five breaths here.

2. Now bring attention to the eyes. What are they doing? What sensations are present? Really feel them. Take five breaths here.

3. Silently choose three words to describe what is present.

4. Now, invite the eyes to *Let go.* Imagine them softening, relaxing and releasing. Take five breaths here.

5. Bring the focus of your awareness next to the tongue and notice any small sensations that arise. The tongue is an extraordinary muscle, which moves in unique ways. Lengthen and shorten it, play with its width, height and shape. Consciously move it around your mouth. Allow it to explore. Take five breaths here.

6. Now, silently choose three words to describe this experience of your tongue. Take five breaths here and then invite the tongue to *Let go.* Feel it soften, relax and release.

7. When ready, transfer the focus of your awareness to the shoulders and describe what you feel. Be curious, specific and detailed in these observations. Now, invite the shoulders to *Let go.* Imagine they are dropping by just a few millimetres. Take five breaths here.

8. Now bring your awareness to the heart and invite it to *Let go.* What happens? Inhale. Exhale. *Let go.* Where is your heart holding on? Inhale. Exhale. *Let go.* Where is your heart ready to release? Inhale. Exhale. *Let go.* Take five breaths here.

9. *Let go. Let go. Let go.* Take five breaths here.

10. On the next breath give your whole body permission to *Let Go.* Take five breaths here.

11. Return to wakefulness in your own way.

Record your experience in your Mindfulness Journal. Note in particular any areas of the body where it was easier or more challenging to *Let Go.*

If practising with others, take turns sharing your discoveries.

# 12 Mindful Movement

## In the midst of movement and chaos, keep stillness inside of you.

DEEPAK CHOPRA

## Invitation

One day at the end of a dance-meditation class one of the participants shared that during the dance she remembered she was involved in a car accident on Monday that week and hurt her arm. It was now Friday evening and she had rushed through the whole week without noticing that she was in considerable pain!

It can be so easy to ignore the body, to override its messages, but at what cost?

This practice is an invitation into a deep experience of body and movement.

## Mindful Tip

To develop this practice, once you have got the hang of the arms, allow other body parts to start moving in time with the breath also. Be creative, see what movement the breath inspires in your hips, chest, legs and feet. Finally, release the whole body into mindful movement.

# PRACTICE 12

Set a timer for five or ten minutes.

Begin by finding a comfortable posture and by bringing your attention to the breath. Take a few moments to let yourself arrive and allow the breath to draw you gently into internal awareness. Allow the gaze to soften, the eyes to close.

1. On each inhalation silently say *In* and on each exhalation silently say *Out.*

2. *In ... Out ... In ... Out ...*

3. Feel the rhythm of the breath inside the body. Become the breath.

4. On the next breath, the arms are going to move up and away from the body on the inhalation and down and back to your sides on the exhalation. The arms do not need to travel far. Just as much as feels comfortable.

5. *In –* arms float up. *Out –* arms float down.

6. As you do this, imagine that the arms are an extension of the lungs, with the same capacity to fill, expand, empty and release.

7. Allow the arms to follow the breath, become the breath, ease the breath and allow the breath to find new expression.

8. Continue until the timer sounds.

9. Return to wakefulness in your own way.

Record your experience of the breath moving the body in your Mindfulness Journal.

If practising with others, take turns sharing your discoveries.

# 13 Nodfulness

Movement has the capacity to take us to the home of the soul, the world within for which we have no name.

ANNA HALPRIN

## Invitation

One summer I spent a blissful week being inspired by the amazing dancer and visionary, Anna Halprin, who at 95 was still teaching, dancing and sharing her vision of a more loving future for humankind.

Some days we spent the whole morning practising moving from standing up to lying down on the floor, something that I never thought I would see a 95-year-old doing unaided.

Anna demonstrated each movement with such grace and instructed us with such a wonderful sense of humour, that each of us was invited into our own body with more courage, compassion and curiosity.

In this practice, see how deeply you can enter into the embrace of your own movement.

## Mindful Tip

To bring additional depth to this exercise, select a piece of calming music to accompany your practice.

# PRACTICE 13

Set a timer for five or ten minutes.

This is a gentle moving meditation that begins in a standing or seated position with the eyes closed. Work within the limitations of your own body. If dizziness is experienced, reduce the movement, pause or sit down and bring your focus back to the breath alone.

1. Stand with the eyes closed and breathe into the whole body noticing the sensations that arise in your awareness.

2. Feel the weight of the head and allow it to become heavy and to drop forward in a slow and controlled way. Let the head fall to a point that feels comfortable without straining.

3. Pause for a moment before allowing the head to return slowly to the upright position.

4. Now connect the breath and this movement together by imagining that it is the breath itself that initiates and creates the movement of your head. As you inhale, the head will rise and on the exhale, the head will fall. Take a break from the movement whenever needed. Keep the breathing measured, relaxed, and even.

5. Continue following this practice allowing yourself to become more and more curious about the physical sensations that arise.

6. Continue until the timer sounds.

Record your experience in your Mindfulness Journal. Many of the sensations that arise within this exercise are subtle so be as accurate and specific in your notes as you can.

If practising with others, take turns sharing your discoveries.

# 14 Mindfulness of Walking

So be sure when you step,
Step with care and great tact.
And remember that life's
A Great Balancing Act.

DR SEUSS

## Invitation

Jacquie is a life coach in Vancouver. She spends many of her sessions walking with clients around the woods and mountains near her home. She says that her clients find it easier to relax and talk about their challenges when they are moving. As they stroll through nature, they become more creative, resourceful and solution-focused.

Walking allows an anxious mind to quieten. Runners report the same thing.

This practice explores the impact of walking on mindful awareness.

## Mindful Tip

'Walking The Space' means allowing everyone in the room to quietly walk around, in any direction, at any speed. The aim is to let everyone wander around, at their own pace, as they become familiar with the room. As they move, the group will take ownership of the space and inhabit it with their energy.

# PRACTICE 14

Make sure the room is adequately spacious for the group, or practise outdoors.

Begin by standing still and bringing your awareness to the breath. Take a few moments to let yourself arrive and allow the breath to draw you gently into internal awareness.

1. Start by Walking The Space (see Mindful Tip).

2. Now, let the gaze drop down a little towards the ground a few metres ahead. Keeping the eyes open, bring the focus of your awareness inward and slow your walking to half-pace. Keep moving forward but with absolutely no hurry. With each step become more present, more aware.

3. Pay close attention to your own body by directing your full focus to the physical sensations of these slow steps. As you do this, notice what you are feeling.

4. Next, practise going between normal walking pace and half-pace. Notice what differences arise in the quality of your awareness when doing so.

5. Now, slow from half-pace to walking as slowly as possible. Decelerate every motion. Slow every footstep. Breathe.

6. How still can you be, whilst keeping the continuous movement flowing?

7. Walking at this pace, what do you feel in your body?

8. For the next few minutes modulate between walking pace, half-pace and slow before bringing the practice to a close in your own time.

Record your experience in your Mindfulness Journal noting in particular anything intriguing that you discovered about your body and its movement.

If you are practising with others, take turns sharing your discoveries.

# 15 Mindfulness of Stretching

## Every experience I've had in my life is a resource in my body.

ANNA HALPRIN

## Invitation

Stretching has somehow become a competitive affair of pushing, striving, and comparing.

What if the limits of physical movements could be witnessed and experienced differently, with a compassionate and kind awareness? What if the body were allowed to open in its own time, in its own way, through listening and attentive presence. What might arise then?

## Mindful Tip

The focus of this practice is the legs but once comfortable with the technique, the same awareness can be brought to any part of the body.

# PRACTICE 15

Set a timer for five, ten or fifteen minutes.

This exercise works best sitting on the floor with the legs stretched out. If that is not possible, choose any comfortable posture where the legs can be stretched within their own comfortable range of movement.

Note that the first instructions do not involve any stretching.

1. Start by feeling your legs up and down with your hands. Within the range of your own easeful movement, make contact with every part of the leg within reach. Squeeze and release. Pat, hold and massage.

2. Experience what it feels like to spend time with your legs. It is rare to engage with the lower limbs in this way, so spend time exploring what they actually feel like. Take five breaths here.

3. Now look carefully at your legs. Acknowledge them. Pay attention to every minute detail and notice something that you have not seen before. Your legs have carried you a great distance. They have taken you on many adventures. They have also brought you into this moment of rest and stillness here today. They are with you now. Be with your legs. Take five breaths here.

4. Now allow the gaze to soften, the eyes to close.

5. Stretch forward slowly and feel the sensations that arise within the legs. Mild discomfort is fine but stop before the stretch becomes painful.

6. Hold the stretch and allow your curiosity to lead you into the specific sensations that are arising. Silently choose three words to describe what you notice.

7. Now move your palms to the part of your leg where you experience the stretch most intensely and make contact (often this will be the back of the knees).

8. At the same time, visualise the breath moving through the body and flowing to the same place. Take five breaths here.

9. Next, release the stretch by sitting back. Take five breaths here.

10. Then, return to the stretch and take five breaths as you gently push forward.

11. What do you notice? Pay particular attention to the sensations in the palms of the hands and to the focus of the stretch in the legs.

12. Repeat the stretch until the timer sounds.

13. Release the stretch and take five final breaths here.

14. Return to wakefulness in your own way.

»

Record your experience in your Mindfulness Journal noting in particular the subtle physical sensations that you noticed in the legs.

If practising with others, take turns sharing your discoveries.

# The Mind

# 16 Meeting Mind

Human beings, by changing the inner attitudes of their minds, can change the outer aspects of their lives.

WILLIAM JAMES

## Invitation

Hold your thumb in front of you and look at it closely. Your thumb is a part of you, but obviously not all of you. What if you could observe mind in the same way?

Cup both hands together in front of you and imagine holding your mind within them. Suppose every thought showed up as a zigzag of light zipping through and every emotion as a cloud of moving colour.

Your mind and the lights passing through, just like your thumb, would not describe all of you either. After all there is the heart, the body, the awareness.

When taking mind as the object of mindfulness practice, the aim is to observe what is there without judgment and to notice that the mind does not describe the fullness of being.

So in this practice welcome mind just as it is, thoughts and all.

## Mindful Tip

Become the observer of the stream of thoughts moving through mind. Do not be afraid of this internal dialogue or its apparent never-ending nature. Engage it with your curiosity. Notice how its activity can coast along without your direction. Sit calmly, watch carefully and see where mind takes you.

# PRACTICE 16

Set a timer for five, ten or fifteen minutes.

Begin by finding a comfortable posture and by bringing your attention to the breath. Take a few moments to let yourself arrive and allow the breath to draw you gently into internal awareness. Allow the gaze to soften, the eyes to close.

1. Bring your focus to the mind and quietly observe what it is doing.

2. The mind is very likely to be carrying a stream of thoughts. The aim of this practice is to be aware of those thoughts without energising them.

   *A thought is energised when followed up with another Intentional Thought, choice, comment, or association or when scheduled for action or added to a to-do list.*

3. At first it can be challenging to disengage the mind's natural tendency to energise thoughts but, with repeated practice and perseverance, it becomes second nature.

4. If you notice that you have energised a thought it is important to practise two things:

   *Non-Judgment, and Self-Compassion.*

5. Non-judgment means that when realising you have energised a thought, you do not treat it as a failure. In fact this realisation is a vital moment within the practice, as you are immediately offered the opportunity to return to the focus of the exercise (i.e. bring awareness back to a neutral observation of mind).

6. Hand in hand with non-judgment comes self-compassion. Being gentle with yourself is necessary because it gradually generates an ability to stay present in quiet observation of mind. If scolding the mind for *messing up* or *doing it wrong* this compassionate awareness is lost.

7. Patiently continue until the timer sounds.

8. Return to wakefulness in your own way.

Record your experience in your Mindfulness Journal noting the subject of thoughts that arise. As you repeat this practice over time, notice if the mind is producing similar or different thoughts as your mindful awareness develops.

If practising with others, take turns sharing your discoveries.

# 17 Naming Thoughts, Emotions and Judgments

## Peace requires us to surrender our illusions of control.

JACK KORNFIELD

### Invitation

Mindfulness practice offers a fresh perspective on how to experience the internal world of awareness which includes thoughts, emotions and judgments. These three elements are frequently present within mind and in this exercise the challenge is to name each aspect as you become aware of it.

### Mindful Tip

By becoming centred in a neutral awareness of the internal workings of mind, perspective can be gained, fears calmed, and the body can relax.

In time the mind itself will become more resourceful and less prone to exacerbating problems through anxious thinking, sometimes referred to as 'catastrophising'.

## PRACTICE 17

Begin by finding a comfortable posture and by bringing your attention to the breath. Take a few moments to let yourself arrive and allow the breath to draw you gently into internal awareness. Allow the gaze to soften, the eyes to close.

1.  Bring your awareness to the mind. There are three things to look out for in turn:

    *Thoughts*
    *Emotions*
    *Judgments*

2.  Begin by naming your thoughts. For example, each time you encounter a thought, silently say:

    *Here is a thought about my day.*
    *Here is a thought about what I will do later.*
    *Here is a thought about this practice.*

3.  Continue for two or three minutes, naming thoughts as they arise, but otherwise adding no energy to each one.

4.  Next, turn your attention to emotions. What do you notice?

5.  Explore by naming emotions as they arise in your awareness:

    *This is sadness.*
    *This is joy.*
    *This is worry.*

6.  Spend two or three minutes noticing your emotions. Resist the urge to analyse why each emotion is present and instead hold it within compassionate awareness.

7.  Finally turn your attention to judgments. Ask yourself:

    *Where am I judging?*

8.  Then, name each judgment as you notice it:

    *I am judging my performance.*
    *I am judging myself.*
    *I am judging this practice.*
    *I am judging life.*

9.  Spend two or three minutes here, noticing if the judgments are punctuated with moments of pause and reflection.

10. Return to wakefulness in your own way.

Record any persistent thoughts, emotions, and judgments in your Mindfulness Journal. If you found parts of the exercise challenging, note this also. Your difficulties are just as useful to learn from as your successes.

If practising with others, take turns sharing your discoveries.

# 18 The Thought Barometer

## What goes up must come down.

ISAAC NEWTON

## Invitation

Creating a link between the mind, body and movement allows a process such as *thinking* to become physical and embodied. In this practice, the movement of the hand up and down will be linked to the passing of thoughts through mind, adding a very physical element to the experience.

When entering this practice, do so without expectation and, as much as possible, release the tendency to judge. The only success measure is showing up and having a go.

Just as air pressure varies day by day, the pressure of thoughts will rise and fall depending on your current state of mind.

## Mindful Tip

With repeated practice longer periods of thought-free awareness are likely to become available.

As the hand movement described in this practice becomes more familiar, you might even find that it is possible to intentionally push your hand down and bring about an experience of thought-free or *silent* awareness.

## PRACTICE 18

Set a timer for five, ten or fifteen minutes.

Begin by finding a comfortable posture and by bringing your attention to the breath. Take a few moments to let yourself arrive and allow the breath to draw you gently into internal awareness. Allow the gaze to soften, the eyes to close.

1. In this exercise the object of contemplation is thought itself.

2. The aim is to notice when a thought is arising and when there is no thought present.

3. It is important to be just as welcoming of the thoughts as the silence. The focus of this practice is simply to be aware.

4. The movement of the hand up and down is used to create a link between the body and the mind. The position of the hand will indicate when thought is present or absent.

5. Begin with one hand on your knee. If you notice a thought, allow the hand to move slowly upwards (stopping at eye level).

6. If you notice a gap between thoughts, allow the hand to slowly fall back down towards the knee.

7. In periods of sustained silence, the hand will rest on the knee until the next thought arises, when it will ascend again.

8. During practice, the hand will either be going up or down, resting on your knee, or resting at eye level.

9. Do not worry if there are very few moments of silent awareness to start with. With repeated practice, the silent periods will increase.

10. Remember that the purpose of this exercise is to notice what the mind is doing with a simple curiosity and without judgment.

11. Continue until the timer sounds.

12. Return to wakefulness in your own way.

Record your experience in your Mindfulness Journal.

If practising with others, take turns sharing your discoveries.

# 19 Intentional Thoughts and Free Thoughts

## The soul becomes dyed with the colour of its thoughts.

MARCUS AURELIUS

## Invitation

Have you ever noticed that there are two types of thoughts: intentional ones that are created by the mind (this is the voice you use to talk to yourself internally) and unintentional thoughts that just seem to bubble up without any effort? For ease of reference I will call the first type Intentional Thoughts and the second type Free Thoughts.

This practice focuses on noticing the differences between Intentional Thoughts and Free Thoughts so that it becomes easier to navigate the sea of data that arises within mind. This in turn supports the skill of being intentional in actions and behaviour.

## Mindful Tip

You are not your Free Thoughts.

Some Free Thoughts can be crazy, mean-spirited, weird and wacky. Do not take them too seriously. Although sometimes they might be useful, often it is best to laugh at their nonsense, letting them fade away.

The trick here is not to cling to Free Thoughts, or to act on them without thinking things through.

# PRACTICE 19

Set a timer for five, ten or fifteen minutes.

Begin by finding a comfortable posture and by bringing your attention to the breath. Take a few moments to let yourself arrive and allow the breath to draw you gently into internal awareness. Allow the gaze to soften, the eyes to close.

1. Start by repeating an Intentional Thought three times. Your thought could be:

   *I am thinking this thought.*
   *I am thinking this thought.*
   *I am thinking this thought.*

2. Now stop and wait.

3. What happens next?

4. If you wait long enough, another thought will arise, but this time it will not have been inserted intentionally in the mind, it will simply have bubbled up from somewhere internally. What was the thought?

5. Let's try that again:

   *I am thinking this thought.*
   *I am thinking this thought.*
   *I am thinking this thought.*

6. Now stop.

7. What happened this time? If a thought bubbled up, what was it?

8. Repeat the practice focusing on any subtle differences that you notice between Intentional Thoughts and Free Thoughts until the timer sounds.

9. Return to wakefulness in your own way.

Record your experience in your Mindfulness Journal noting the differences you sensed between Intentional Thoughts and Free Thoughts.

If practising with others, take turns sharing your discoveries.

# 20 Repetition or Mantra

## Meditation means to be constantly extricating yourself from the clinging mind.

RAM DASS

## Invitation

Mantras have been used in meditation for thousands of years as a method to enter deeper states of awareness.

A mantra is a repeated phrase that holds an important meaning or resonance for the subject. The act of repeating a mantra over and over, allows the mind to settle into periods of peaceful awareness, absent of thought.

Anyone can create a mantra by selecting a short phrase that holds personal meaning. Ideally the mantra should be made up of words that have a nice rhythm and an appealing sound, such as:

*The stillness resides in me.*
*Peace within and all around.*
*Breathing, smiling, letting go.*

## Mindful Tip

Vary this practice by speaking the mantra out loud. How does this change your experience?

# PRACTICE 20

Set a timer for five, ten or fifteen minutes.

Begin by finding a comfortable posture and by bringing your attention to the breath. Take a few moments to let yourself arrive and allow the breath to draw you gently into internal awareness. Allow the gaze to soften, the eyes to close.

1. Centre yourself in your breathing.

2. Silently repeat your mantra over and over. Allow the pace to flow organically. Sometimes it might be fast, sometimes slow, unhurried, even ponderous. At all times it should feel easy and natural.

3. Now, let the meaning of the words subside and allow the sounds that make up each word to be the focus of your attention.

4. When the mind wanders, patiently come back to the sounds of the words of your mantra.

5. Allow the sounds to gather and resonate within you.

6. Feel the vibrations of every syllable.

7. On each repetition, imagine you are hearing the mantra for the first time.

8. Repeat until the timer sounds.

9. Return to wakefulness in your own way.

Record your mantra and your experience of this meditation in your Mindfulness Journal.

If practising with others, take turns sharing your discoveries.

# 21 Mind the Gap

When one past thought has ceased
and a future thought has not yet risen,
in that gap, in between, is not there a
consciousness of the present moment
... a luminous, naked awareness?

SOGYAL RINPOCHE

## Invitation

If you have ever been to London and travelled on The Tube
(the underground train network) you know that one of the
most often-heard announcements is *Mind the Gap* which
draws attention to the sometimes large chasm between
carriage and platform.

In this practice by drawing attention to the gaps between
thoughts, comfort in thought-free awareness grows, even if
the gaps are only present for a nanosecond.

## Mindful Tip

Try Practice 19 before attempting this one as it introduces
the concept of Intentional Thoughts and Free Thoughts.

## PRACTICE 21

Begin by finding a comfortable posture and by bringing your attention to the breath. Take a few moments to let yourself arrive and allow the breath to draw you gently into internal awareness. Allow the gaze to soften, the eyes to close.

1. Bring your attention to the mind and notice the Free Thoughts that are naturally arising.

2. Allow the Free Thoughts to be present and as they move into your awareness see if you can spot the gaps in between them.

3. Spend a minute or two here welcoming and acknowledging both the gaps and the thoughts.

4. Now, spend a minute or two paying close attention to the body. Can you discern any subtle difference in feeling or awareness when a thought is present to when it is absent?

5. Next when noticing a thought coming through, see if you can slow down the words of the thought, as if listening to a really slow recording.

6. Treat this as a game and employ your patience and curiosity in discovering how to slow thoughts down. Take five breaths here.

7. Next, slow the thoughts down even further so that little gaps become visible between the words themselves. Spend a minute or two experimenting here.

8. Now try the same things with an Intentional Thought such as

   *I am thinking this thought*
   *I_am_thinking_this_thought_*
   *I__am__thinking__this__thought_*
   *I___am___thinking___this___*
   *thought__*

9. Repeat your Intentional Thought another five times, each time slowing it down.

   *I am thinking this thought*
   *I_am_thinking_this_thought_*
   *I__am__thinking__this__thought_*
   *I___am___thinking___this___*
   *thought__*
   *I___am___thinking___this___*
   *thought___*

10. How slow can you go?

11. What do you notice about your experience in the gaps?

12. Return to wakefulness in your own way.

Record what you noticed in the gaps in your Mindfulness Journal.

If practising with others, take turns sharing your discoveries.

# 22 Meeting the Inner Critic

You have been criticising yourself for years and it has not worked. Try approving of yourself and see what happens.

LOUISE L HAY

## Invitation

The Inner Critic is never far away. Within the internal world of thought, the Inner Critic is often lurking in the shadows of mind, ready to offer a scolding comment, a cutting insult, or condemn behaviour.

Having an Inner Critic is normal: *Believing* the Inner Critic is madness.

In reality, the Inner Critic is a fearful fellow who rarely sees the whole picture. By holding his voice in the context of wider awareness, it becomes second nature to notice when his contributions are unfounded and untrue.

There is no need to live in fear, or in reaction, to the Inner Critic. Instead, make a practice out of noticing when his voice is present, reminding yourself that you do not need to take his comments too seriously.

## Mindful Tip

The Inner Critic's voice is subtly distinct from others that you might hear internally. Learn to identify it by listening closely for its tone of voice or a particular feeling that accompanies it.

For those with a tendency to self-judge, take this practice slowly. Be gentle with yourself and remember that whatever comes up can be welcomed with compassionate awareness.

As you get to know the Inner Critic, this practice can be extended by asking the Inner Critic questions such as:

*What is your purpose?*
*Who are you?*
*Why do I hear your voice?*
*What do you need?*

## PRACTICE 22

Begin by finding a comfortable posture and by bringing your attention to the breath. Take a few moments to let yourself arrive and allow the breath to draw you gently into internal awareness. Allow the gaze to soften, the eyes to close.

1. Centre yourself in your breathing and allow the body to move into gentle alignment.

2. Bring to mind a thought or situation where you feel conflicted, fearful or are struggling such as:

   *I wish I was in better shape.*
   *Please let my presentation go well.*
   *I hate finding parking in the city.*

3. Now make space for and welcome any negative self-judgments, thoughts and comments. Listen closely.

4. As the criticism arises, notice what occurs in mind. Take five breaths here.

5. What happens in your body? Take five breaths here.

6. What happens to the breath? Take five breaths here.

7. Now, ask the Inner Critic to tell you more about how you are failing.

8. Whilst listening, choose three words to describe the Inner Critic's voice. Take five breaths here.

9. Next see if you can answer the following questions:

   *Does the voice sound male or female?*
   *Is the voice associated with someone you know?*
   *What does your Inner Critic look like?*

10. You might get an abstract response like seeing a colour or feeling an emotion. All responses are valid. Greet whatever comes as exactly what you need in this moment.

11. Now, imagine that you are able to step back and view the Inner Critic from a distance. Take five breaths here.

12. Finally, take five breaths into your heart as you offer the Inner Critic the full strength of compassionate awareness.

13. Return to wakefulness in your own way.

Record your experience in your Mindfulness Journal noting any specific qualities of the Inner Critic that you gathered during the practice.

If practising with others, take turns sharing your discoveries.

# 23 Questioning Thoughts

## An unquestioned mind is the world of suffering.

BYRON KATIE

## Invitation

Troubling thoughts are little parcels of wisdom wrapped up in fear.

Stressful thoughts can only let go and unravel when questioned.

Just like at Christmas, the unwrapping is half the fun!

## Mindful Tip

This exercise is best practised alone in a space where you will not be overheard.

If that is not possible, the exercise can also be done silently.

# PRACTICE 23

Begin by finding a comfortable posture and by bringing your attention to the breath. Take a few moments to let yourself arrive and allow the breath to draw you gently into internal awareness. Allow the gaze to soften, the eyes to close.

1. Find a thought that is bothering you and say it out loud, repeating it over and over again; e.g.

   *I am alone.*
   *I am alone.*
   *I am alone.*
   *I am alone.*
   *I am alone.*

2. As you do so, focus on the sounds that make up each word and let their meaning drift away.

3. Allow these sounds to fill your curiosity.

4. As you continue your repetitions at some point, the words will change.

5. Allow this to happen without questioning where the words are going and without attaching any meaning to the new words.

6. Repeat the new words, listening to them and sensing in your body whether they feel wise or silly, profound or nonsensical. Make room for all the words without judgment.

7. Keep playing. Let the words change again.

8. Sometimes the words will repeat, sometimes they will pass through quickly.

9. Continue the associations until the words have all passed through and you are left in stillness.

10. Return to wakefulness in your own way.

Record your experience in your Mindfulness Journal noting any of the phrases and words that particularly resonated, or intrigued you.

# 24 The Knowing Mind

Our deepest fear is not that we are inadequate. Our deepest fear is that we are powerful beyond measure. It is our light, not our darkness that most frightens us.

MARIANNE WILLIAMSON

## Invitation

Each of us gets to play many different roles in life: student, teacher, child, parent, client, advisor, seeker, guide ... the list goes on. Parents and teachers typically speak from the knowing mind whilst child and student are more likely to speak from the unknowing mind.

Beyond the simplicity of whether knowledge is present or absent, there is something about adopting a role that gives the mind permission to know.

This practice plays with the idea that there is always access to both the Knowing Mind and the Unknowing Mind.

## Mindful Tip

After each answer, record your *knowings* in your Mindfulness Journal. Do not worry if not all of the content is useful. A little knowing, goes a long way!

# PRACTICE 24

This is a spoken exercise to do in pairs. One person will be 'A' and the other 'B'. For clarity, read the instructions twice before beginning and make sure that each person has pen and paper.

1. A and B begin by writing down on a sheet of paper three questions that they currently find troubling such as:

   *Why am I still single?*
   *Why do I seem to be failing at this?*
   *Why am I sick?*

2. Now exchange your list of questions and make sure you can read them.

3. Then, connect with your partner by taking a few moments with gentle eye contact and taking five deep breaths. Inhale and exhale together.

4. Next, A says to B: You have full permission to speak from your Knowing Mind.

5. Then, A reads out B's first question switching 'I' for 'you' where necessary); e.g.

   *Why am 'I' still single?* becomes:
   *Why are 'you' still single?*

6. B's job is to listen to the question as if hearing it for the first time.

7. Having posed the question, A now becomes completely quiet and listens deeply, silently welcoming whatever B wishes to share.

8. B now engages the Knowing Mind and speaks from the part of themselves that *knows*. To do this, they have full permission to *know* and they should not worry whether the words that come are true or right. They can talk as freely as possible as if connected to all of the knowing in the Universe.

9. Consider any information that comes up to be research or reconnaissance.

10. When B has completed their answer, A acknowledges B by saying:

    *Thank you for sharing your knowing with me.*

11. B now has time to make any notes of the answers in their Mindfulness Journal. A can help them remember what they said.

12. Now it is B's turn to ask and listen. Repeat the process following instructions 4–11 but swapping roles.

13. Repeat until all the questions have been answered.

Share with each other what you learned through this practice.

# 25 Welcoming the Inner Sage

I'm a believer in fate and in fulfilling your destiny. I've always had a kind of inner voice that I have learned to listen to.

TOM FORD

## Invitation

Practices 19 and 21 play with Intentional Thoughts and Free Thoughts. The Inner Sage is yet another stream of data available within the internal world of consciousness.

The Inner Sage speaks from a place of wisdom and intuitive knowing. Her voice is quiet, gentle and calm. As the Inner Sage rarely shouts, in order to hear her you have to get really quiet within.

## Mindful Tip

As familiarity with this practice grows, reflect on this question:

*Is the Inner Sage part of me, separate from me, or both?*

# PRACTICE 25

Begin by finding a comfortable posture and by bringing your attention to the breath. Take a few moments to let yourself arrive and allow the breath to draw you gently into internal awareness. Allow the gaze to soften, the eyes to close.

1. Begin by noticing the mix of Intentional Thoughts and Free Thoughts that are present within mind.

2. Now allow a question to arise. Perhaps something that is currently troubling you.

3. Hold the question clearly in your awareness and set a direct intention to be available to hear the Inner Sage.

4. Take five deep breaths.

5. Focus on a welcoming energy, allow the mind to be curious, the body spacious.

6. Listen deeply.

7. Gather any and all responses noticed: sensations, images, feelings, thoughts, words, ideas.

8. When sensing the Inner Sage, take note of her qualities. What does the interaction feel like? What is your relationship to the Inner Sage?

9. Now, silently choose three words to describe the Inner Sage to more easily recognise her again.

10. If it feels natural, offer gratitude and appreciation to the Inner Sage for any insights.

11. Return to wakefulness in your own way.

Record your experience in your Mindfulness Journal noting the qualities of the Inner Sage and if you feel inspired, draw an image that represents her.

If practising with others, take turns sharing your discoveries.

Part B

# APPLYING MINDFULNESS IN DAILY LIFE

# Daily Practices

# 26 Mindful Mornings

The ordinary acts we practise every day at home are of more importance to the soul than their simplicity might suggest.

THOMAS MOORE

## Invitation

This practice was inspired by Dr Christine Carter's 'Better-Than-Nothing Workout' consisting of a one-minute plank, 20 push-ups, and 25 squats which she does every morning upon waking. She says this three-minute daily practice has significantly contributed to her overall health.

What would your Better-Than-Nothing morning routine be?

Here are some suggestions to help build your own.

## Mindful Tip

There are five stages to this practice but feel free to start with one or two, or even a different one each weekday. Get creative and see what sticks. The aim is to create an enjoyable morning practice which fits into your busy schedule and which you return to day after day.

# PRACTICE 26

## STAGE 1 – Breathe

1. Pay close attention to your first breaths of the day.

2. Set your timer for one, three or five minutes and on each breath add a count to the inhale and exhale. In your head it sounds like this: *One, one. Two, two. Three, three, etc.*

## STAGE 2 – Stretch

3. Bend, yawn, fold and open.

4. Allow the body to teach you today's unique stretching routine.

5. Now shake and jump until energy is flowing through every cell.

## STAGE 3 – Strengthen

6. Do ten repetitions of three exercises that you already know well and which require no equipment. Be present and aware through each movement.

   • _____
   • _____
   • _____

## STAGE 4 – Sit

7. Set a timer for your mindfulness meditation. Choose anything between one and twenty minutes.

8. As your object for meditation choose one from this list:

   • Self: sit in gentle awareness of that which is arising within you.
   • My Day: contemplate the day ahead.
   • Appreciation: notice all of the things that you feel grateful for in this moment.
   • A person you love.

## STAGE 5 – Commit

9. Complete the following sentences by speaking them aloud or writing them in your Mindfulness Journal. Do not think too much about each one, just say what comes in the moment:

   a. Today I am committed to: _____
   b. Today I will make my contribution by: _____
   c. Today I am most grateful for: _____
   d. Today I let go of: _____
   e. Today I forgive: _____

Record your experience, along with your commitments, in your Mindfulness Journal.

# 27 Dressing Mindfully

## Fashion is instant language.

MIUCCIA PRADA

### Invitation

The clothes you wear and how you wear them silently declare your identity, ethics and style.

Here is a practice to allow your wardrobe to really speak your language.

### Mindful Tip

If your mornings are busy and hurried, consider doing this practice before going to bed or whilst in the shower!

# PRACTICE 27

Begin by finding a comfortable posture and by bringing your attention to the breath. Take a few moments to let yourself arrive and allow the breath to draw you gently into internal awareness. Allow the gaze to soften, the eyes to close.

1. Visualise the day ahead and take five breaths whilst considering:

   *What am I doing today?*
   *Who am I going to see?*
   *Where will I be going?*

2. Make space in your awareness for the delightful surprises and mystery that will interweave itself with your planning. Take five breaths here.

3. Now silently choose three words that express how you want to feel journeying through your day today; e.g.

   Comfortable. Elegant. Creative.

4. Now open your eyes and contemplate your wardrobe as if meeting it for the first time.

5. Stand in the full awareness of your creativity and allow yourself to observe what is in front of you.

6. Now, let the hands choose new combinations, unexpected pairings, and surprising additions.

7. Play and experiment until your look declares everything you want it to say.

8. Finally, if you are prone to over-accessorising, take one thing off. Less is more.

Note the pieces that made up today's outfit and your experience of the process of finding it in your Mindfulness Journal.

# 28 Mindfulness Cues

## A single conscious breath is a meditation.

ECKHART TOLLE

## Invitation

Research shows that mindfulness is most effective when practised regularly and frequently.

As practise deepens it is useful to bring the mindful awareness generated during morning or evening practice into the rest of the day.

The following practice aims to integrate reminders to pay attention to the present moment into your everyday.

## Mindful Tip

The Mindfulness Cues described in this practice point towards living life in the spirit of the unending meditation.

Change Mindfulness Cues frequently in order to keep this practice engaging and new.

# PRACTICE 28

## STAGE 1 – Learning the Conscious Breath and the Mindful Minute

### The Conscious Breath

1. Before inhaling, centre yourself in the intention to take a conscious breath.

2. Inhale slowly, allowing the full focus of awareness to be on the physical sensations of the breath.

3. As the inhale peaks and then slows, witness the small pause that precedes the exhale.

4. Now slowly exhale with full presence attending on each and every physical sensation. Ride the exhalation as it dissolves into silent thin air.

### The Mindful Minute

1. Set a timer for one minute.

2. Bring the attention to the breath.

3. Focus carefully on one, or more, of the physical sensations of breathing. Perhaps choose the rise and fall of the belly, or the passage of air in and out of the nostrils.

4. Count how many breaths are taken before the timer goes off.

   *One inhalation plus one exhalation = one breath.*

5. Now you know how many breaths are taken in one minute, gift yourself a Mindful Minute anytime you choose.

## STAGE 2 – Picking your first three Mindfulness Cues

1. Your Mindfulness Cues are going to prompt either a Conscious Breath or a Mindful Minute; your choice.

2. First select three Mindfulness Cues:

   - One Sound: e.g. the phone ringing
   - One Object: e.g. a post box
   - One Person: e.g. your nemesis

3. Each time a Mindfulness Cue arises in your day, simply take a Conscious Breath or Mindful Minute.

Record your Mindfulness Cues in your Mindfulness Journal.

## STAGE 3 – Extending your cues

1. If this helps, consider adding further Mindfulness Cues.

2. Here are some more examples:

   - One Task: e.g. tying your shoelaces
   - One Place: e.g. your front door
   - One Journey: e.g. your commute
   - One Meal: e.g. breakfast
   - One Day: e.g. Monday

Record further Mindfulness Cues in your Mindfulness Journal.

# 29 Mindful Writing

## Life itself is the most wonderful tale.

HANS CHRISTIAN ANDERSEN

## Invitation

This practice is inspired by the work of David Benjamin Tomlinson, Creative Intuitive Coach and Writer, who teaches his clients to connect with the stream of creative consciousness that opens in the space of deep listening. The process can be both revealing and healing.

If challenging issues arise within your writing, consider working with the support of a friend or a professional.

## Mindful Tip

Some people enjoy this as a morning practice whilst others find it easier at the end of the day. Experiment and see what works best.

# PRACTICE 29

Open your Mindfulness Journal and take a few moments to simply let yourself arrive. Allow the breath to draw you into presence.

1. Set a timer for five, ten or fifteen minutes or select a number of pages to fill today.

2. Take five breaths and welcome the arising flow of words.

3. Now write, whatever comes.

4. You can write *anything*.

5. It does not have to be about something.

6. It just has to be words.

7. They do not even need to be real words.

8. Let the letters tumble free.

9. Give the words your full attention.

10. Follow where they lead.

11. Breathe into the flow.

12. Listen as you write.

13. Get out of your own way. The analytical mind is not required in this game.

14. Breathe.

15. When the timer goes, or your pages are complete, stop and notice what you are feeling.

16. Acknowledge the flow of energy that has moved through during the practice. How has your body, mind and breathing changed since the beginning of the exercise?

If it feels right, read the pages back to yourself and record any further reflections. It is also perfectly fine to simply close your Mindfulness Journal and return to your day.

If working with a friend or a professional, consider if you wish to share your words with them and perhaps discuss what came up within this practice.

# 30 Mindful Shower or Bath

In one drop of water are found
all the secrets of all the oceans;
in one aspect of you are found
all the aspects of existence.

KAHLIL GIBRAN

## Invitation

The ritual of cleansing the body is a beautifully rich daily
practice that is already built into the framework of each
day. By dedicating this time to mindful awareness, more
than just the body can be purified.

## Mindful Tip

For regular practice, note the elements of this exercise,
laminate it and stick it to the bathroom wall!

# PRACTICE 30

These are beautiful rituals to gift yourself at the beginning or end of the day.

## Shower

The shower is a perfect place for meditation. Whatever time is available, you can use the shower as a way of cleansing body and mind and reinvigorating yourself.

1. Step into the shower and spend a few moments with eyes closed.

2. Connect with the feeling of water running over the body.

3. Visualise the water as rejuvenating energy bringing healing and vitality to every cell of your body. Take five breaths here.

4. Now stand comfortably, letting the water connect with the crown of the head. Take five breaths here.

5. Visualise the water as energy moving directly into the head and down into the body. Notice what sensations, images, feelings and thoughts arise. Take five breaths here.

6. Let the visualisation dissolve.

7. Next, cleanse the body with your hands bringing the full focus of awareness to each body part in turn and washing away any tension.

8. In every moment is a new beginning: body and mind are refreshed, cleansed, made new.

9. Let the movements of your hands communicate loving care and compassion as you connect physically with the body.

10. Finally, turn the temperature down and allow the cooler water to bring stillness to body and mind. Take five breaths here.

Record your reflections in your Mindfulness Journal.

## Bath

Read through the instructions in full and prepare everything needed for your bath in advance, so that once the water begins to flow, full attention can be paid to the practice.

1. Begin by setting your intention creatively. Here are some examples:

   - *I offer my ritual in gratitude for all that I am and all that I have.*
   - *Through this ritual I generate love and healing in my life.*
   - *By this ritual I open to the adventure of today.*

2. Now commence the flow of water, watch it fall, tumble, swirl and pool within the bath. Pay close attention and allow your awareness to be drawn into gentle observation of the chaos that arises at the beginning of something new.

»

*Acknowledge one aspect of your life that is currently chaotic.*

3. As the water gets deeper, notice how it is still in motion but the surface is able to rest in greater stillness.

   *Acknowledge one aspect of your life that is calming.*

4. Once the bath is full, turn off the water and watch.

   *Notice one aspect of your life where something has stopped.*

5. Remembering your intention, enter the bath and allow the water to hold you. Notice the physical sensations of temperature, flow, texture and closeness. Take five breaths here.

   *Close the eyes for a moment and reflect on one aspect of life where you are supported.*

6. Rest in the water noticing you are held by a substance that the body cannot survive in for long.

   *Notice one aspect of your life where you feel out of your comfort-zone.*

7. Then, cleanse the body with the hands, bringing the full focus of awareness to each body part in turn and washing away all tension.

8. In every moment is a new beginning: body and mind are refreshed, cleansed, made new.

9. Let the movements of your hands communicate loving care and compassion as you connect with your physical form.

   *Acknowledge one thing you are ready to leave behind.*

10. Before climbing out of the bath, place your hands on any part of the body that is calling for attention. Take five gentle healing breaths.

11. Exit the bath and before removing the plug watch the gentle motion of the water caused by your departure.

    *As you pull the plug and allow the bath to empty, reflect on one aspect of life where you are moving on.*

12. As the last gurgles of water drain away, close your ritual by rinsing the bath and appreciating yourself for taking time for this practice.

Record your reflections and inspirations in your Mindfulness Journal.

# 31 Gratitude Rituals

Piglet noticed that even though he had a Very Small Heart, it could hold a rather large amount of Gratitude.

A A MILNE

## Invitation

It turns out that gratitude is the secret to joy.

## Mindful Tip

Listen to Piglet. That is all.

»

# PRACTICE 31

## Gratitude Journal

1. Find a beautiful little notebook to be your Gratitude Journal or use the Mindfulness Journal that you already have.

2. At the start or end of each day write down three things that you are grateful for.

3. Repeat daily.

## Gratitude Stone

1. Find a small stone that holds particular significance. It could be a gemstone, a pebble from the beach or one that turns up in the garden or even on the street.

2. Each morning put the stone in your pocket or handbag. Every time something happens in your day that you are grateful for, touch the stone and silently say: *Thank you.*

3. At the end of the day, place the stone in a special place and as you put it down, remember and appreciate all of the wonderful things that happened today.

## Gratitude in the mail

1. At a frequency of your choosing (say once a week or once a month) send someone in your life a thank you note or email.

2. Be specific, tell them what they did for you, how it helped, what changed, and why it was important for you to communicate your appreciation.

3. Mix things up by occasionally sending yourself a letter of thanks.

## Advanced gratitude

It is easy to be grateful for the things that are wonderful. It is hard to be grateful for our challenges, issues, obstacles and perceived enemies.

1. In your Gratitude Journal start adding one further entry each day that relates to something challenging that you are grateful for, and the reason why.

2. If using a Gratitude Stone, occasionally touch the stone when something difficult happens. At the same time locate something positive you can be grateful for in the situation such as:

*I am grateful this situation has passed.*
*I am grateful I am strong enough to deal with this.*
*I am grateful I have friends to turn to.*

# 32 Mindful Tea / Coffee Break

Drink your tea slowly and reverently as if it is the axis on which the world Earth revolves – slowly, evenly, without rushing toward the future.

THICH NHAT HANH

## Invitation

Breaks in the day are often accompanied by emails, social media, advert-laden magazines and other distractions meaning that the mind is still busy working away.

This practice is a reminder of how to *really* stop.

## Mindful Tip

Take Mindful Breaks in unusual settings and locations. This does not mean you have to climb the nearest mountain or rest on an escalator: even sitting in a chair that you normally would not choose, or finding a different park bench is enough. Originality of experience increases ability to be present.

»

## PRACTICE 32

A Mindful Break means a full pause without any technology or distraction. Let it be one human being, one drink and some time and space to simply *be*.

1. Do whatever is needed in order to feel comfortable disconnecting from technology for the length of your break.

2. Prepare your favourite drink and take it to a restful spot. It could be the sofa, a park bench, or the old chair in the garden. Get really comfortable; this is not a meditation posture so curl up, pull a blanket over if you like, and relax.

3. Hold the mug close and breathe. Deeply inhale.

4. Let go completely and exhale. Sink into the seat. Sink into the peacefulness of this moment. Sink into the now.

5. Allow yourself to land fully in the freedom of these moments dedicated to noticing what is arising within.

6. Take a sip.

7. How do you feel?

8. Take another sip.

9. What do you notice in your body?

10. Another sip.

11. What thoughts are bubbling up in your mind?

12. Let all of it be just as it is, and breathe. Deep, open, calming breaths.

13. Drink. Contemplate. Be.

Record the feelings, sensations and thoughts from your practice in your Mindfulness Journal.

# 33 Practical Kindness

Thousands of candles can be lit from a single candle, and the life of the candle will not be shortened. Happiness never decreases by being shared.

GAUTAMA BUDDHA

## Invitation

Notice how you are always in the right place at the right time.

## Mindful Tip

Trust your body, if being asked for help by a stranger and your immediate response is fear, the appropriate action is to walk away.

»

# PRACTICE 33

Here are three ways to change the course of history today!

## VARIATION 1 - The gift

1. Buy a gift for a stranger.

2. Perhaps it is a sandwich for a homeless person, a treat for a new co-worker or the book you just finished for the person sitting next to you on your way to work.

3. Notice what sensations, images, feelings and thoughts arise as you contemplate your gift and then make your offering.

4. In your Mindfulness Journal record how this action changed your day and notice any ripple effect on those around you.

## VARIATION 2 - Generosity

1. Give a little money to someone who needs it more than you today.

2. Allow the gift to be pure, clean and unconditional.

3. With the giving of the gift, smile and experience the impact of your generosity.

4. Notice what it feels like to act on your compassion.

## VARIATION 3 - Serving others

1. Be of service today.

2. Offer to carry your neighbour's groceries, hold a door open, help someone in need across the road.

3. If you see someone in distress, stop and ask how you can help.

4. Smile and connect with an open heart.

5. What happens?

Record your experience in your Mindfulness Journal noticing what is changing in your life as you experiment with these simple practices.

# 34 Maximising Energy

If you want to find the secrets of the Universe, think in terms of energy, frequency and vibration.

NIKOLA TESLA

## Invitation

Energy follows thought.

## Mindful Tip

Some people are more naturally sensitive to the energies of places, people and things than others. For those who are peculiarly sensitive, their experience of the World can be very confusing. The egg exercise helps all of us maintain clear energetic boundaries and sense external energies in a useful way.

»

# PRACTICE 34

Begin by finding a comfortable posture and by bringing your attention to the breath. Take a few moments to let yourself arrive and allow the breath to draw you gently into internal awareness. Allow the gaze to soften, the eyes to close.

## The egg

1. Sit comfortably imagining yourself to be inside a large glowing egg of white light.

2. Allow the energy flowing through the egg to regenerate the energy of the body.

3. Notice how the light circulates through your body and then back into and around the egg.

4. Your breath connects your energy to the egg. Take five breaths as you see and feel this connection.

5. Practise this visualisation until the egg can be clearly seen and you feel supported by its rejuvenating energy.

## Permission settings

6. Permission settings can be added to the egg through the clarity of your intention.

7. Your intention may be:

   *The egg maximises my energy*
   *The egg shields me from depleting energies.*
   *The egg rejuvenates me.*

## Further settings

8. It is possible to extend the egg exercise by setting an intention for the egg to be present and operative throughout the day until it is deactivated.

9. Alternatively, set an intention for the egg to activate, in an instant, at full strength whenever needed.

10. If setting an activation intention, it will be useful to create a physical prompt or anchor for this in the body; e.g.

    *Pressing thumb and middle finger together activates the egg.*

11. For the anchor to be effective, you will need to practise the visualisation whilst holding finger and thumb in the anchor position.

12. Return to wakefulness in your own way.

Record your experience in your Mindfulness Journal. Note in particular any differences that you notice in your interactions with others as you gain familiarity with this practice.

# 35 Noticing Five Things

## 80% of success is just showing up.

WOODY ALLEN

## Invitation

Be where you are.

## Mindful Tip

Here is a worked example to demonstrate this practice.

*Mary was sitting at the train station waiting for the train. She noticed:*

1. The little bumps on the ground that alert blind people to the fact that they are close to the platform edge. Mary felt happy to live in a world where compassion is shown in this way.

2. The wind was brisk and a little cold. Mary considered putting her jacket on.

3. Looking up Mary noticed a stunning cloud in the sky above the station. Multi-layered, multi-coloured, lit as if by a master of visual effects. Mary was in awe.

4. Mary noticed her bag beside her. A trusty brown leather handbag filled with everything imaginable. It reminded her of her travels, her work and her children.

5. The train was now arriving, calling Mary's attention with its growls and hisses. Mary smiled, knowing that she would soon be home.

»

# PRACTICE 35

No need to worry about posture. Just breathe and look around.

1. Take a few calming breaths and centre yourself in the present moment.

2. Allow your attention to be drawn to five things in turn. Remember, there are no success measures, so follow your curiosity. You can notice anything!

3. Your attention comes to rest on your first object.

   *What is it?*

4. Check in with your body and be present to the subtle sensations moving through you.

   *What feelings and thoughts arise as you contemplate this?*

5. Take five breaths here to simply be present with your first object.

6. Repeat four more times.

Note your reflections on your Five Things and record your experience of this practice in your Mindfulness Journal.

# Welcoming the Good

# 36 Slowing Down

There is more to life than simply increasing its speed.

MAHATMA GANDHI

## Invitation

There was a day after leaving my career as a barrister that I stopped tying my shoelaces so tight. Every morning, before setting off for court, I had yanked on those tiny strings, ensuring my feet had no chance of escape.

That day, as I took off my trusted black leather shoes, I noticed that my feet were hurting; my skin bore the imprint of the shoe. I had not noticed before but I am certain, it had been the same for years.

If you invite the Energy of Slow into your life, you will find more and more ways to loosen your laces.

## Mindful Tip

In a world of speed dating, express checkouts, fast tracks and lightning-speed wifi, it is easy to forget that important parts of life thrive on the Energy of Slow.

# PRACTICE 36

Begin by finding a comfortable posture and by bringing your attention to the breath. Take a few moments to let yourself arrive and allow the breath to draw you gently into internal awareness. Allow the gaze to soften, the eyes to close.

1. You have arrived. Focus on the feeling of welcoming and take five slow breaths here.

2. Notice if the activity of your day is still buzzing around inside the mind. What thoughts, images, memories, feelings, sensations and emotions have followed you into your practice?

3. Acknowledge the whirl of activity that the mind is still chewing over as you begin your practice. Observe it neutrally and welcome it by allowing it to be just as it is. Know that it will settle in its own time.

4. Offer your breath an invitation to *Slow Down* and take five easeful breaths here.

5. Now, bring the same invitation to the body: *Slow Down*.

6. Take five breaths as the Energy of Slow circulates gradually through every bone, every muscle, every artery, every cell.

7. Next, take the focus of your awareness to mind and offer it the invitation: *Slow Down*.

8. Now wait and observe. As the mind renews its activity, offer the invitation again: *Slow Down*.

9. Take five breaths here and before bringing your practice to a close, contemplate how the Energy of Slow can be welcomed into daily life.

10. Return to wakefulness in your own way.

Record memorable sensations, images, feelings and thoughts in your Mindfulness Journal and note three areas of your life where the Energy of Slow might be beneficial.

If practising with others, take turns sharing your discoveries.

# 37 Contentedness Practice

Happiness is when what you think, what you say, and what you do are in harmony.

MAHATMA GANDHI

## Invitation

Happiness is a daily skill.

Whilst there is always something to complain about, equally there is always something to be happy about. It comes down to where you choose to place your focus in any moment and how you want to experience life.

By building on happy experiences that are already present during the day and adding in a dash of gratitude and accomplishment, a more contented outlook can flourish.

## Mindful Tip

Happiness does not grow on trees; it grows on little moments like this one.

# PRACTICE 37

Begin by finding a comfortable posture and by bringing your attention to the breath. Take a few moments to let yourself arrive and allow the breath to draw you gently into internal awareness. Allow the gaze to soften, the eyes to close.

1. Let the breath welcome you into your practice. Take five calming breaths here.

## Happiness

2. Bring your attention to something that made you feel happy today.

   *What happened?*

3. Return fully to the memory.

   *Where are you?*
   *What is occurring?*
   *Who are you with?*

4. Take five breaths here as you re-experience the situation and invite the energy of happiness in.

5. *What was it about the situation that brought happiness?* Examine the memory and feel the feelings of happiness again. Breathe into the feelings and watch them grow. Make the memory brighter and more vivid. Sense it moving through your body. Take five breaths here.

6. When ready, allow that memory to gently subside.

## Gratitude

7. Next, direct your attention to something that you felt grateful for today.

   *What was it?*

8. Return fully to the memory.

   *Where are you?*
   *What is occurring?*
   *Who are you with?*

9. Take five breaths here as you re-experience the situation and invite the energy of appreciation in.

10. *Why did you feel grateful?* Examine the memory and feel the feelings of gratitude again. Breathe into the feelings and watch them grow, make the memory brighter and more vivid. Sense it moving through the body. Take five breaths here.

11. When ready, allow that memory to gently subside.

## Accomplishment

12. Bring your attention to something practical that you accomplished today.

    *What was it?*

13. Return fully to the memory.

    *Where are you?*
    *What is occurring?*
    *Who are you with?*

»

14. Take five breaths here as you re-experience the situation and invite the energy of accomplishment in.

15. Reflect on the memory and feel the feeling of accomplishment again. Breathe into the feeling and watch it grow, make the memory brighter and more vivid. Sense it moving through the body. Take five breaths here.

16. When ready, allow that memory to gently subside.

17. Having felt the energy of happiness, gratitude and accomplishment in turn, now allow yourself to feel the combination of all three flowing in the body. Take five breaths here.

18. Silently choose three words that describe how you feel now.

19. Return to wakefulness in your own way.

Record your chosen three words in your Mindfulness Journal and reflect on how your experience evolved through the practice.

If practising with others, take turns sharing your discoveries.

# 38 Growing Compassion

## If we have no peace, it is because we have forgotten that we belong to each other.

MOTHER TERESA

## Invitation

Experiencing and growing the energy of love and compassion is a traditional focus for mindfulness practice. In this exercise the focus of compassionate awareness moves from the self to a loved one, to someone in need, to a challenging individual and finally to all living things. In this way, compassion moves outwards from the centre of personal experience into the World.

## Mindful Tip

Become adept at offering compassion to yourself first, no matter how counter-intuitive this may feel.

Without developing the craft of self-compassion, compassion for others will remain weak.

»

# PRACTICE 38

Begin by finding a comfortable posture and by bringing your attention to the breath. Take a few moments to let yourself arrive and allow the breath to draw you gently into internal awareness. Allow the gaze to soften, the eyes to close.

1. The stillness of your awareness welcomes your breath into the heart.

2. Breathe deeply and connect with heart. Feel its abundance. Sense its wisdom.

3. On your next breath, silently repeat *I am compassion* five times:

   *I am compassion.*
   *I am compassion.*
   *I am compassion.*
   *I am compassion.*
   *I am compassion.*

4. Take five breaths here noticing what occurs in your awareness as the statement echoes through.

5. Be your experience.

6. Welcome what is arising with curiosity.

## Self

7. Now bring your attention to a challenging aspect of life. *What is it?* How does it make you feel? What emotions come up as you contemplate the situation?

8. Place both hands on your heart and offer yourself the gift of your own abundant compassion. Take five breaths here.

9. Hold yourself and the challenge within compassionate awareness. Be with yourself. Offer yourself comfort.

10. Attend to yourself with acceptance, love and patience. Take five breaths here.

## A loved one

11. Now bring to mind a loved one. Someone close and dear. Visualise them with you, feel their energy, sense their presence and offer them the bounty of your compassion.

12. Stay with the energy. Observe what occurs, noticing transitory sensations, images, feelings and thoughts.

13. Take five breaths breathing here in loving awareness.

## Someone in need

14. Next bring to mind a person or group of people who are in need.

15. Call them to mind. Visualise being with them and offer them the gift of your compassionate awareness.

16. Stay with the energy. Observe what occurs noticing transitory sensations, images, feelings and thoughts.

17. Take five breaths here.

## A challenging individual

18. Now, call to mind someone you find challenging. Hold them in your awareness and offer the energy of compassion.

19. If difficult emotions arise, place both hands on the heart and take five deep breaths.

20. Stay with the energy. Observe what occurs, noticing transitory sensations, images, feelings and thoughts.

21. Take five breaths here.

## All living things

22. Finally, bring to mind all living things by visualising planet Earth. Hold the life of this planet in your awareness and offer the energy of loving compassion.

23. Stay with the energy. Observe what occurs, noticing transitory sensations, images, feelings and thoughts.

24. Take five breaths here.

25. Return to wakefulness in your own way.

Record your experience of each stage of this practice in your Mindfulness Journal.

If practising with others, take turns sharing your discoveries.

# 39 Accessing Intuition

Don't try to comprehend with your mind.
Your minds are very limited.
Use your intuition.

MADELEINE L'ENGLE

## Invitation

The main sense organs of most insects are the antennae.
These long, slender projections are covered with tiny
sensitive hairs and they enable the insect to feel, smell and
sometimes taste, and hear.

In this practice, the visualisation of antennae growing from
the forehead is used as a method of enhancing intuition.

## Mindful Tip

On subsequent attempts try gently rubbing the third-eye
area of your forehead with your finger for 10 seconds before
attempting the practice and see if anything changes in
your experience.

The focus of this practice is intuitive awareness of another
person but you can easily create variations by changing
the focus to anything you wish such as: a current challenge,
a creative project, or a social issue.

# PRACTICE 39

Begin by finding a comfortable posture and by bringing your attention to the breath. Take a few moments to let yourself arrive and allow the breath to draw you gently into internal awareness. Allow the gaze to soften, the eyes to close.

1. Allow the breath to lead you into an expanded awareness of the body. Spend time feeling for specific sensations of weight, temperature, pressure, tension and comfort in turn. Gently scan the body.

2. Now, bring your attention to the head and imagine two small bumps starting to form on your forehead. Take five breaths here as you feel and see your antennae growing.

3. As the antennae emerge from your forehead and grow taller and longer, notice what colour they are, and if they have a texture. Take five breaths here.

4. Your antennae are now fully formed. What shape are they? How long are they? What does it feel like to carry them on your head? Take five breaths here.

5. Now, without effort, bring to mind a key person in your life, visualise them in front of you. See them clearly. Take five breaths here.

6. Focus now on your antennae and with a deep acknowledgement of your own intuition, bring your attention to that person fully.

7. Allow your sense of compassion to grow and take five breaths here.

8. Now, see if you can sense their emotional state. Take five breaths here.

9. Next, bring your attention to anything that person wishes to communicate with you. Take five breaths here.

10. Make space within the silence of your intuitive awareness to welcome any further information that your antennae is receiving. Take five breaths here in deep listening.

11. Finally, if there is anything that you wish to communicate to the other person, do so now. Take five breaths here.

12. When the practice feels complete, allow the antennae to shrink and disappear as the visualisation fades.

13. Return to wakefulness in your own way.

In your Mindfulness Journal record your intuitive insights.

If practising with others, take turns sharing your discoveries.

# 40 Abundance

## Acknowledging the good that you already have in your life is the foundation for all abundance.

ECKHART TOLLE

### Invitation

Within the inner world of felt bodily sensations lies the seat and source of abundance.

### Mindful Tip

Whenever you feel depleted, come back to the abundant energy of the body and remind yourself of the vibrant expression of living life that is your physical form.

# PRACTICE 40

Begin by finding a comfortable posture and by bringing your attention to the breath. Take a few moments to let yourself arrive and allow the breath to draw you gently into internal awareness. Allow the gaze to soften, the eyes to close.

1. Connect with the breath and invite in the full presence of awareness. Drop deeply into this moment and notice the sensations that are arising within.

2. Take five full breaths and experience the frequency of life resonating in the body.

3. Allow the physicality of this experience to be increased. Feel it more.

4. Notice that there is a vibration to this experience. Silently choose three words to describe what you feel.

5. Continue breathing here until you can sense even the smallest vibration of life in the body.

6. Now imagine the same vibration in every cell. Take five breaths here.

7. Feel the body teeming with the energy of abundance.

8. Acknowledge this abundance that lies within you.

9. Take five breaths here.

10. Return to wakefulness in your own way.

In your Mindfulness Journal, record a description of what the energy of abundance feels like.

If practising with others, take turns sharing your discoveries.

# 41 I Am Enough

## What lies behind us and what lies before us are tiny matters compared to what lies within us.

OLIVER WENDELL HOLMES

## Invitation

This practice is inspired by the author Marisa Peer who speaks about the incredible transformations in the lives of her celebrity clients when they started living by the simple affirmation:
*I am enough.*

She encourages all to take those three little words home, to write them on notes around the house, to set up daily reminders on every device and to draw it on the mirror with lipstick or soap!

See what happens when you remind yourself of the simple truth that you are indeed, enough.

## Mindful Tip

In today's media-dominated world it is easy to be infected by feelings of scarcity and imperfection.

This simple practice is a reminder that everything you need to navigate the now is neatly packed inside you and accessible in the present moment.

# PRACTICE 41

Begin by finding a comfortable posture and by bringing your attention to the breath. Take a few moments to let yourself arrive and allow the breath to draw you gently into internal awareness. Allow the gaze to soften, the eyes to close.

1. Centre yourself and let the breath draw you into quiet contemplation.

2. With each inhalation embrace who you are in this moment.

3. With each exhalation let go of anything that no longer serves you.

4. Take five breaths repeating the embrace and the letting go.

5. Now, silently repeat to yourself the affirmation *I am enough* five times:

   *I am enough.*
   *I am enough.*
   *I am enough.*
   *I am enough.*
   *I am enough.*

6. Notice any sensations, images, feelings and thoughts that arise. Take five breaths here.

7. Next, repeat *I am enough* five more times, but this time allowing the voice to be gently heard as a whisper.

8. Notice any sensations, images, feelings and thoughts that arise. Take five breaths here.

9. Then, at normal conversation volume repeat *I am enough* five more times.

10. Pay particular attention to any impulses within the body.

11. Notice what changes, what comes forward in your awareness.

12. Take five breaths here.

13. Cycle through the exercise twice more.

14. Return to wakefulness in your own way.

Record the sensations, images, feelings and thoughts that came from this affirmation practice in your Mindfulness Journal.

If practising with others, take turns sharing your discoveries.

# 42 When / Then What?

If you are depressed, you are living in the past. If you are anxious, you are living in the future. If you are at peace, you are living in the present.

LAO TZU

## Invitation

When/Then statements are ways of placing things that are desired, such as happiness, out of reach. Examples include:

**When** I have a boyfriend, **then** I will be fulfilled.
**When** I get that job, **then** I will be happy.
**When** I earn more money, **then** I will be safe.

This practice reminds us that fulfilment, happiness and safety can all be located in the present moment without a change in circumstances.

## Mindful Tip

Once you start noticing your own When/Then statements, keep a list of them in your Mindfulness Journal.

As you realise how this way of thinking has separated you from joy and happiness, an opportunity arises to practise self-compassion and forgiveness and to set a new commitment to finding joy in the here and now.

# PRACTICE 42

Before beginning, read the Invitation and Mindful Tip and make a list of three When/Then statements to take into your practice.

Begin by finding a comfortable posture and by bringing your attention to the breath. Take a few moments to let yourself arrive and allow the breath to draw you gently into internal awareness. Allow the gaze to soften, the eyes to close.

1. Centre yourself in your practice and let the breath invite you into the contemplation of your first When/Then statement; e.g.

   **When** *I have a boyfriend,* **then** *I will be fulfilled.*

2. Take five breaths here as you notice any sensations, images, feelings and thoughts that arise.

3. Contemplate the following questions:

   *What are the consequences of believing the statement?*
   *What am I keeping myself apart from?*

4. Now consider where in life you already experience what you are seeking (*e.g. fulfilment*). Silently name all the things present in your life right now that give rise to that feeling. Take five breaths here.

5. Breathe in the knowing: you have everything you need.

6. Repeat the process for your second and third When/Then statements.

7. Return to wakefulness in your own way.

For each When/Then statement now record in your Mindfulness Journal at least one new statement that is true, or truer. For example:

Original: **When** *I have a boyfriend,* **then** *I will be fulfilled.*

New: *I am fulfilled now and I do not currently have a boyfriend.*
*I find fulfilment in my work, my family and my friends.*

If practising with others, take turns sharing your discoveries.

# 43 Enhancing Sports Performance

Impossible is potential.
Impossible is temporary.
Impossible is nothing.

DAVID BECKHAM

## Invitation

To lift the trophy once in your hands, you must lift the trophy
every day in your heart and mind.

## Mindful Tip

Variations of this exercise can easily be created in order
to make it applicable to any skill or ability you wish
to enhance.

# PRACTICE 43

Begin by finding a comfortable posture and by bringing your attention to the breath. Take a few moments to let yourself arrive and allow the breath to draw you gently into internal awareness. Allow the gaze to soften, the eyes to close.

1. Contemplate the sporting skill you wish to develop. Take stock of your current strengths and weaknesses just as they are. Take five breaths here.

2. Now call to mind your hopes and dreams. What is your ideal outcome? Dream big. Do not be constrained in this vision by any thought of impossible. Give yourself full permission to shine brightly. Take five breaths here.

3. On the next breath, imagine a time in the future when you have become a master of your sport. As this image gathers in your awareness, allow the details to come into clearer focus.

4. Hold this vision of mastery in your awareness, breathing into its vivid detail.

5. Silently describe the specifics of what you see.

   *How far in the future is it?*
   *What do you look like?*
   *What clothing are you wearing?*

6. Zoom in on any details that are calling your attention. Take five further breaths and explore.

7. Take your time to now consider the following:

   *What do you see in the image that you do not currently have?*
   *How was this mastery achieved?*
   *If this future self could offer advice, what would it be?*

8. Listen deeply and breathe.

9. If there is an important match or championship ahead, visualise yourself having won. Hear the sounds of support surrounding you. See the joy on your own face. Feel the trophy in your hands. Lift it high. Celebrate your win. Take five breaths here.

10. Now allow the visuals to fade and watch the benefits of this vision being absorbed into the body. Let every cell vibrate with the buzz of mastery, joy and celebration.

11. Return to wakefulness in your own way.

Record your experience in your Mindfulness Journal noting in particular any intriguing answers that arose in response to instruction 7.

If practising with others, take turns sharing your discoveries.

# 44 Me 2.0

## You are the Universe, expressing itself as a human for a little while.

ECKHART TOLLE

### Invitation

Let your future self whisper in your ear, and allow life to unfold of its own accord

### Mindful Tip

This exercise can be useful at times of confusion and change. Remember that looking back on life it will be easier to plot the journey and make sense of the path. In this moment, trust in the perfection of that which is unfolding.

# PRACTICE 44

Begin by finding a comfortable posture and by bringing your attention to the breath. Take a few moments to let yourself arrive and allow the breath to draw you gently into internal awareness. Allow the gaze to soften, the eyes to close.

1. Settle into the rhythm of your breath, allowing the passage of the outside world and the movements of the day to fade into the background. Take five breaths here.

2. See yourself in the future.

3. In this future image you feel free, your body moves easefully, there is less tightness. There is no need to hold on as you have relaxed into a sense of joy and ease.

4. The mind feels clear. The heart is open. Wherever you are, you are surrounded by love and appreciation. You are valued, seen, heard and fully supported. Take five breaths here.

5. In this future, you are doing what you love. You were destined for this. You are making your contribution and bringing your unique vision to the World.

6. You are happy, healthy, strong and vital. You feel energised, dynamic, bold and confident.

7. More than this, you notice a new depth to your compassion and loving. You feel light.

8. Explore the sensations of this future and silently choose three words that will anchor this vision. Take five breaths here.

9. Now look around:

   *Where are you in the world?*
   *How far in the future is it?*
   *Who is with you?*
   *What are you doing?*
   *What clothing are you wearing?*
   *Where do you live?*

10. Take five further breaths as you make your discoveries.

11. Follow your curiosity and listen deeply.

12. Now ask the future version of yourself if it has a message for you? Take five breaths and listen deeply.

13. Send appreciation and love to your future self and allow the vision to recede.

14. Return to wakefulness in your own way.

Record your experience in your Mindfulness Journal noting in particular any intriguing answers that arose in response to instruction 9 and 12.

If practising with others, take turns sharing your discoveries.

# Difficult Days

# 45 Returning to Centre

Within yourself is a stillness, a sanctuary to which you can retreat at any time and be yourself.

HERMAN HESSE

## Invitation

The centre within this practice is a place of powerful inner silence reached through quiet contemplation. It is the still point: the fulcrum of awareness.

As the journey back to centre becomes more familiar, experiment with speaking, acting and creating from this place.

Life can easily throw you off centre. This practice will help you find the way back.

## Mindful Tip

When repeatedly striking the chest, imagine knocking at the door of your awareness.

# PRACTICE 45

Begin by finding a comfortable posture and by bringing your attention to the breath. Take a few moments to let yourself arrive and allow the breath to draw you gently into internal awareness. Allow the gaze to soften, the eyes to close.

1. Place an open palm on your upper chest where it feels almost flat. Take five breaths here focusing on this single point of contact.

2. Now gently start to pat your chest with the palm. Allow each impact to shake off the tensions of the day. Set an intention that each beat will lead you closer to your centre. Take five breaths here.

3. Find a rhythm and intensity that feels strong yet comfortable.

4. Notice how the body is being called into presence and observe how the mind responds. Take five breaths here.

5. Notice how the sound of each impact affects your awareness. Take five breaths here.

6. Without counting, strike your chest about one hundred times.

7. Feel your awareness being drawn to your centre.

8. When you feel present, clear and ready allow the strikes to slow down to a gentle stop and allow your hand to gently fall and rest comfortably.

9. Take five breaths here in silent stillness.

10. Listen in gentle awareness of your centre until your practice feels complete.

11. Return to wakefulness in your own way.

Record your experience in your Mindfulness Journal detailing anything you have revealed about your centre. If you feel inspired, draw an outline of the body and pinpoint your centre. Draw how the body feels right now.

If practising with others, take turns sharing your discoveries.

# 46 Accepting Emotions

## What you resist persists.

ECKHART TOLLE

### Invitation

Emotions are like the weather of internal awareness. As the old saying goes: *You cannot stop the waves, but you can learn to surf.*

This practice introduces a staged process for welcoming difficult emotions mindfully and uncovering the wisdom they might contain.

### Mindful Tip

If you have a creative outlet like painting, drawing, writing, dance or photography, take lingering emotions into your artwork, movement, music or journal. If not, do a doodle.

# PRACTICE 46

Begin by finding a comfortable posture and by bringing your attention to the breath. Take a few moments to let yourself arrive and allow the breath to draw you gently into internal awareness. Allow the gaze to soften, the eyes to close.

## Accept

1. When difficult emotions are inviting attention, begin by acknowledging that there is a choice: to listen, or ignore.

2. Just for this moment, find a way to accept your emotional state exactly as it is, no matter how challenging.

## Welcome

3. Welcome the presence of emotion within your awareness and allow yourself to really feel the sensations that arise. Take five breaths here.

4. Notice whether the mind resists feeling the sensations of this emotion. Take five breaths here.

5. Include within your awareness the experiential feeling of the emotion in your body.

6. Let this emotion have its way with you. Take five breaths here.

## Express

7. Now it is time to move the emotion into expression by giving it a sound.

8. Whether it is a wail, a sigh, a whisper, laugh or a scream, let this emotion be heard. (Do not worry if the expression is neither pretty nor cool.)

## Be courageous

9. Locate your courage and remind yourself of the strength you hold within. Take five brave breaths here.

## Listen

10. Emotions bring wisdom. Make space to listen for the teaching that has accompanied this emotional state. Take five breaths here.

11. Are you being called in to a different decision? Are you feeling the outcome of a prior choice? What learning is available in this moment?

12. Listen deeply as you take five breaths here.

## Integrate

13. Integrate the wisdom of this emotion into the body and awareness.

14. Finally, notice whether the emotion and your own feelings towards it have changed.

15. Return to wakefulness in your own way.

Record the wisdom of your emotions in your Mindfulness Journal.

If practising with others, take turns sharing your discoveries.

# 47 Down Days

Even a happy life cannot be without
a measure of darkness, and the word
'happiness' would lose its meaning
if it were not balanced by sadness.

CARL JUNG

## Invitation

It is easier to fall into a hole than to climb out of it, but if you
exit with grace, you may find yourself less afraid of falling.

## Mindful Tip

Your track record for getting through tough days so far is
one hundred per cent. You will also get through this one.

Remember, you have every reason to have faith in yourself.

# PRACTICE 47

Begin by finding a comfortable posture and by bringing your attention to the breath. Take a few moments to let yourself arrive and allow the breath to draw you gently into internal awareness. Allow the gaze to soften, the eyes to close.

## STAGE 1 - Exploration

1. However you are feeling right now, breathe into it and silently name what is arising within.

2. Inhale into the challenge and notice what degree of emptiness, sadness and futility is present. Imagine yourself to be in a deep hole.

3. Give all your challenging feelings full permission to be present with you in the hole and take five breaths here.

4. Access your curiosity and imagination and look all around. Take five further breaths.

5. *How large is the hole? What colour is it? Where is it?*

6. Silently choose three further words to describe your current experience.

## STAGE 2 - Perspective

7. Now, imagine that your awareness could float upwards out of the hole. By ascending you can look down on the situation from a bird's eye view.

8. From above, the path taken into the hole can be seen.

   *What do you notice about how you got here?*

   Take five breaths here.

9. *Where did you think the path was leading?*

   Take five breaths here.

10. *What choices, agreements and actions were taken that led to this experience?*

    Reflect and take five further breaths.

11. Now look a little way ahead, in front of the hole and see the paths that lead away from there.

12. Notice something unexpected.

13. As you observe the paths ahead:

    *Which path feels most easeful, joyful and inviting?*

    Take five breaths here.

»

## STAGE 3 - Analysis

14. Now open your eyes and write your answers to these questions in your Mindfulness Journal. Do not overthink your responses, write whatever comes first without worrying whether it is right, true or your complete best answer:

- *What have I lost sight of?*
- *What part of myself am I neglecting?*
- *Which of my values have I compromised?*
- *Where have I stopped learning?*
- *What agreements have I broken?*

If practising with others, take turns sharing your discoveries.

# 48 Mindfulness of Anger

Holding on to anger is like grasping a hot coal with the intent of throwing it at someone else; you are the one who gets burned.

GAUTAMA BUDDHA

## Invitation

Treat anger like any other object of contemplation by welcoming it, observing it and offering it your genuine curiosity.

In the space of awareness anger may dissolve into pure wisdom.

## Mindful Tip

It is normal for difficult emotions to arise during this exercise so ensure that there is plenty of time to process whatever emerges from your practice. There is no rush.

When you are ready, anger will be waiting, bearing gifts.

»

# PRACTICE 48

Begin by finding a comfortable posture and by bringing your attention to the breath. Take a few moments to let yourself arrive and allow the breath to draw you gently into internal awareness. Allow the gaze to soften, the eyes to close.

1. Take five courageous breaths in acknowledgement of your commitment to meet your anger.

2. Set an intention to welcome anger into your awareness with compassion.

3. Now, complete the following sentences out loud with as much freedom as you can. Each starter phrase may lead to a single word, a few lines, or a five-minute monologue. No need to think about the answers in advance, just let yourself go and give voice to what is there.

   *I am angry that ...*
   *I am angry with ...*
   *I am angry because ...*
   *I am angry for ...*
   *I am angry about ...*

4. Let the words tumble out. It may take seconds, minutes or longer.

5. If the words did not flow freely, repeat instructions 1–4 until anger has been fully heard.

## Optional continuation

6. If it feels appropriate, repeat the following phrase five times:

   *I am not my anger.*
   *I am not my anger.*
   *I am not my anger.*
   *I am not my anger.*
   *I am not my anger.*

7. Pay close attention to any sensations, images, feelings and thoughts that arise. Take five breaths here.

8. Return to wakefulness in your own way.

In your Mindfulness Journal record and reflect upon any key phrases that came through in the spoken part of the practice.

# 49 Anxious Thoughts

## Fear: the best way out is through.

HELEN KELLER

### Invitation

Fear inhibits the flow of awareness. Luckily, the breath has an amazing ability to release the mind's attachment to anxious thoughts and to transform fear into ease.

Although the natural reaction to fear is to hold on more tightly, when it comes to living life mindfully, there can be no safety in clinging, only peace in free fall.

### Mindful Tip

This practice can be further developed by choosing a third colour to symbolise positive thoughts. Start by observing them and instead of dissolving them, increase them using your intention and the breath.

»

# PRACTICE 49

Begin by finding a comfortable posture and by bringing your attention to the breath. Take a few moments to let yourself arrive and allow the breath to draw you gently into internal awareness. Allow the gaze to soften, the eyes to close.

1. Take ten deep breaths. Inhale fully, exhale fully.

2. Next, take ten further breaths and allow the natural rhythm of your breathing to return.

3. Gradually let the awareness of your breathing fade into the background.

4. Bring your attention to an anxious thought or thoughts, be they profound or superficial.

5. Choose a colour to symbolise anxious thoughts within your body. Take five breaths here.

6. Imagine this colour is highlighting all the places in your body where you feel stress and anxiety to be present. Watch and observe. Take five breaths here.

7. *Which parts of your body light up? Where is the colour most obvious, most intense?*

   Take five breaths here.

8. Now notice if the colour is moving or static? Is it hot or cold? Does the colour have a texture?

9. Silently choose three words that describe what you notice.

10. Next, place both hands on the heart and sense the reservoir of compassion within the body. Take five breaths here.

11. Notice how bringing your awareness to compassion allows it to well up within your body and to flow throughout.

12. Choose a colour to symbolise your compassion and observe it flowing through your body. Notice how effortlessly and easefully it moves. Take five breaths here.

13. Next observe how the flow of compassion in the body has affected the anxious thoughts.

    *What has changed?*
    *What colours are now present?*

14. Now, consciously breathe into any areas of the body where anxiety is still present. Set an intention that within the presence of your compassion the anxiety may dissolve.

15. Take ten conscious breaths and observe.

16. Repeat the ten breaths until you feel calm, peaceful and centred.

17. Return to wakefulness in your own way.

Record your experience in your Mindfulness Journal noting how your experience of anxiety has evolved through this practice.

If practising with others, take turns sharing your discoveries.

# 50 Mindfulness of Pain

## Nothing happens to any man that he is not formed by nature to bear.

MARCUS AURELIUS

### Invitation

Pain comes in all shapes, flavours, consistencies and sizes. Whether your pain is emotional, physical, mental or spiritual, allow this practice to lead you towards a new awareness of it.

Tangled within pain may be found a tricky invitation to deepen self-compassion and open to inner wisdom.

### Mindful Tip

Go slowly with this exercise and if your pain is intense or extreme, consider working with a close friend or a professional.

## PRACTICE 50

Begin by finding a comfortable posture and by bringing your attention to the breath. Take a few moments to let yourself arrive and allow the breath to draw you gently into internal awareness. Allow the gaze to soften, the eyes to close.

1. Offer pain the full focus of your awareness and take five deep breaths here.

2. Sense whether you are holding on to a story about your pain such as:

   *Poor me. Life is bad.*
   *I should not be in pain.*
   *I cannot live with this pain.*
   *Why me?*

   Acknowledge any element of story that may be active and just for now, let your awareness of the story fade. Take five breaths here.

3. Now, bring your full attention to a pure experience of the felt sensations of your pain, just as they are. Welcome this experience by accepting it fully just for this moment. Take five breaths here.

4. Allow yourself to really feel the pain itself. Feel it deeply, specifically, tangibly. Meet it fully.

5. Focusing next on attending with compassion, stay with these feelings for a further five breaths and listen.

6. Explore the pain as if experiencing it for the first time. Silently choose three words that best describe the pain. Avoid judgments like *awful* or *horrific* but instead pick descriptive or visual words such as *burning* and *piercing*.

7. Next, ask yourself:

   *Where in my body does pain reside?*

8. As you contemplate this question, notice if your hands are drawn to certain places on the body. Allow the hands to attend caringly. Do not worry if they are drawn somewhere unexpected, trust your intuitive wisdom. Take five breaths here.

9. Imagine now that there is a volume dial for your pain, which can be turned up or down.

10. Turn the dial up ever so slightly.

    *What happens?*

    Now turn it down a little.

    *What changes?*

11. Play with the dial for the next 10 breaths, perhaps seeing how effectively you can reduce your experience of pain.

»

119

12. Finally, breathe and offer your pain the full depth of your listening.

    *What would my pain tell me if it had a voice?*

    *What does my pain want me to know?*

    Take five breaths here.

13. Silently name one thing that has been learned about pain in this practice. Take five further breaths.

14. Return to wakefulness in your own way.

Record what you have discovered about the experience of pain in your Mindfulness Journal. Even if you only notice very subtle shifts in perception, record them diligently.

If practising with others, take turns sharing your discoveries.

# 51 Forgiveness Meditation

## Dumbledore says people find it far easier to forgive others for being wrong than being right.

J K ROWLING

### Invitation

When forgiveness seems out of reach, here is an invitation to locate the deepest source of self-compassion within.

### Mindful Tip

This can be a difficult and powerful practice. Allow time following the exercise to process fully by writing about your experience in your Mindfulness Journal. If you feel unable to deal with the emotions that come up, seek help from a trusted friend, or a professional.

»

# PRACTICE 51

This is a spoken meditation, which is best practised alone with eyes open or closed.

Begin by finding a comfortable posture and by bringing your attention to the breath. Take a few moments to let yourself arrive and allow the breath to draw you gently into internal awareness.

1. Breathe until you feel calm, clear and ready.

## STAGE 1 - Self

2. Complete the following sentence and repeat it at least three times until it feels authentic, truthful and clear:

   *I forgive myself for …*

3. Now repeat the following phrase at least three times until it feels true or truer:

   *I accept myself as I am.*
   *I accept myself as I am.*
   *I accept myself as I am.*

4. Finally declare at least three times:

   *I am released.*
   *I am released.*
   *I am released.*

## STAGE 2 - Other

5. Complete the following sentence and repeat it at least three times until it feels authentic, truthful and clear:

   *I forgive (insert name) for …*

6. Now repeat the following phrase at least three times until it feels true:

   *I accept (insert name) as they are.*

7. Finally declare at least three times:

   *I am released.*
   *I am released.*
   *I am released.*

## STAGE 3 - Life

8. Complete the following sentence and repeat it at least three times until it feels authentic, truthful and clear:

   *I forgive life for …*

9. Now repeat the following phrase at least three times until it feels true:

   *I accept life as it is.*
   *I accept life as it is.*
   *I accept life as it is.*

10. Finally declare at least three times:

    *I am released.*
    *I am released.*
    *I am released.*

11. Return to wakefulness in your own way.

Record your experience in your Mindfulness Journal. Note in particular shifts you notice in the body, emotions and sensations as you move through each stage.

# 52 Mindfulness of Failure

## Live life as if everything is rigged in your favour.

RUMI

### Invitation

Failure is the most faithful of all teachers.

### Mindful Tip

Note in your Mindfulness Journal three failures from your past that you now look back on with relief.

»

# PRACTICE 52

Begin by finding a comfortable posture and by bringing your attention to the breath. Take a few moments to let yourself arrive and allow the breath to draw you gently into internal awareness. Allow the gaze to soften, the eyes to close.

1. Contemplate a specific failure, take five welcoming breaths.

2. Relax any tight areas in the body that are calling for attention. Remind yourself that you can let go. Take five breaths here.

3. Now, allow the eyes to open and write your responses to the following questions in your Mindfulness Journal.

   What was the intended goal?

   How did you fail?

   What three words describe your feelings in relation to this failure?

   Identify one aspect of yourself that was not ready to succeed? (If this is hard, close your eyes and listen deeply for five breaths.)

   What has this failure strengthened?

   What have you learned from this failure?

   What does this failure make space for in your life?

   What has not changed despite this failure?

If practising with others, take turns sharing your discoveries.

# 53 Letting Go of the Past

Someone I loved once gave me a box full of darkness. It took me years to understand that this too, was a gift.

MARY OLIVER

## Invitation

The past cannot hurt you, but how you think about your past can destroy you.

## Mindful Tip

Adapt this meditation to add particularly important junctions in your own life.

Find your own way home.

»

# PRACTICE 53

Begin by finding a comfortable posture and by bringing your attention to the breath. Take a few moments to let yourself arrive and allow the breath to draw you gently into internal awareness. Allow the gaze to soften, the eyes to close.

1. Spend a few moments in gratitude for this breath and allow a sense of appreciation for the life you have lived to build in every cell of your body. Take five breaths here.

2. In this practice, there is an invitation to journey inward, through your past, as witness.

3. From a bird's eye view you can watch the unfolding drama of your personal history.

4. As you do so, hold an attitude of appreciation and notice that every step was leading you here to this moment of stillness, calm and perspective. Take five breaths here in preparation.

5. On your next breath, journey to your very first memories of childhood.

6. There may be glimpses of your parents, your siblings, early travels, your home, bedroom, first friends, favourite toys, the view from your window.

   What do you see?
   What do you feel?

7. Look down in gratitude. Find something new to appreciate. Take five breaths here.

8. Now a little older, you find yourself at school. There is your desk, your friends, the faces of teachers, your school bag, those lunches. Remember the ups and downs of tests, making friends, the jokes, the highs and the lows.

9. Look around carefully. Enjoy the view. Find something new to appreciate and take five breaths here in grateful appreciation.

10. On the next breath you find yourself a little older. You are starting to have an idea of what you are going to do, and who you would like to be. Maybe there are more exams, perhaps things are changing, and you may be moving away from home.

11. Notice your growth, your maturing, all the battles, triumphs, achievements and failures that brought you to your first moments of independence. Find something new to appreciate and take five breaths here in grateful appreciation of your struggles and successes.

12. It is now later still and an adult relationship comes to mind. This was a difficult time when you experienced conflict and tension. Take five breaths here as you acknowledge the strength that you found and the lessons learned.

13. Find something new to be grateful for as you notice who you were becoming within this challenging relationship.

14. Come back now to the present time and reflect on your journey. Notice how everything always leads you to this moment now. Sense how a very long and winding road has already led you home.

15. Breathe in gentle gratitude for the life you have lived and acknowledge the wisdom collected on this journey.

16. Return to wakefulness in your own way.

Record all the new things you found to appreciate in your Mindfulness Journal.

If practising with others, take turns sharing your discoveries.

# Visualisation Journeys

# 54 The Path

It's good to have an end to journey toward,
but it's the journey that matters in the end.

URSULA K LEGUIN

## Invitation

Visualisation is another way to explore the arena of
internal awareness.

## Mindful Tip

Remember that all of the senses can be used during
visualisation practice so if you find it challenging to picture
the journey described, feel what it would be like to be there,
sense the environment, smell the forest, hear the sounds.

# PRACTICE 54

Begin by finding a comfortable posture and by bringing your attention to the breath. Take a few moments to let yourself arrive and allow the breath to draw you gently into internal awareness. Allow the gaze to soften, the eyes to close.

1. The journey begins high up in the mountains. As you turn you are met by the most beautiful snow-laden peaks majestically rising upwards to meet the clarity of the deep blue sky. All around the snow stretches out like a glistening blanket of winter promise. Take five breaths here.

2. The cool fresh air enters your nose and travels into your lungs whilst the warmth of the sun embraces your cheeks. You feel grateful for your winter clothes, sturdy boots and the provisions in your bag.

3. The path seems to be leading down the mountain. You take your time on the rough terrain and gradually work your way downwards. Take five breaths here.

4. You find yourself following a tiny flow of melt water whose patient travels have carved a stream in the mountain rock.

5. With each twist and turn of the path the stream becomes a little wider and a little deeper. You follow, joyfully breathing in the sunshine, the clean cold air and the magnificent views. Take five deep breaths here.

6. You hear the gentle thundering of what must be a waterfall ahead. Excitedly you stride on, turning the corner to see a lake fed by not one, but five waterfalls all tumbling playfully into the clear blue of this wonderful pool. Take five breaths here.

7. Without thinking, you undress and jump straight in. To your surprise the water is warm and healing! You paddle, swim, jump and submerge, playing like a child until you feel refreshed, cleansed, peaceful and healed. Climbing out to dry in the sun, you take five breaths here.

8. Dressed and ready, the path calls you once again. It follows the small river that emerges from the lake, taking the water onwards down the mountain. There is a little boat, which you sense has been left on the bank just for you. You board and paddle it forward down the gentle river and into the forest ahead. Take five breaths here.

9. The light plays on the water as you enter the forest, the sun glistening through the gentle dance of the leaves above. The trees bow towards the river as you glide through, feeling their wisdom, their stillness, their love. Take five breaths here.

10. As you emerge from the forest and the river widens, you arrive at the sandy shore where the river emerges into the sea.

»

11. The boat lands on the beach and you pull it up the shore to rest. As you climb out and lie down, you allow yourself to be held by the warm white sand. Take five breaths here.

12. It is dark now, the stars are glistening in the sky above, the moon is glowing. You rest in gratitude for the simplicity of your day, the beauty of the journey, for who you have become and where you have been. Take five grateful breaths here.

13. Return to wakefulness in your own way.

    Reflect on the following questions and record your answers in your Mindfulness Journal.

    *Am I on my path?*
    *Where am I going?*
    *Am I making the most of where I am now?*

If practising with others, take turns sharing your discoveries.

# 55 Strengthening the Core

## Pain is inevitable, suffering is optional.

HIS HOLINESS, THE DALAI LAMA

### Invitation

You did not come into this world, you came out of it.

If that is true, your stardust-body-mind must know a thing
or two about the deepest secrets of life.

### Mindful Tip

As you tune into the magnetism within each cell, follow
the flow of energy up and down.

»

# PRACTICE 55

Begin by finding a comfortable posture and by bringing your attention to the breath. Take a few moments to let yourself arrive and allow the breath to draw you gently into internal awareness. Allow the gaze to soften, the eyes to close.

1. Take five deep breaths into the belly and ground yourself in the experience of this moment. Ask yourself:

   *How centred do I feel?*
   *How grounded do I feel?*
   *How strong do I feel?*

2. Now, imagine magnetic energy spiralling above your head, moving down through the centre of the body and exiting through your seat.

3. Breathe into the spiral: watch and feel it moving within. Take five breaths here.

4. Become even more deeply absorbed in this energy and curious about its sensations. Take a further five breaths.

5. Now, imagine that every tiny cell of the body is aligning and vibrating in response to the spiral of magnetic energy moving in your body. Take five breaths here as you notice what occurs.

6. Stay with the visualisation and take five breaths into your centre.

7. Keeping the breath measured and present, ask yourself:

   *Where is my core?*
   *How do I experience my core?*

8. Take five breaths here.

9. Listen deeply:

   *What does your core awareness ask you to know in this moment?*

   Take five breaths here.

10. On the next breath ask yourself:

    *How centred do I feel?*
    *How grounded do I feel?*
    *How strong do I feel?*

11. Return to wakefulness in your own way.

Record any resonant answers that came to you through this practice in your Mindfulness Journal.

If practising with others, take turns sharing your discoveries.

# 56 The Tree House

## With a tree house and a little imagination we can go anywhere!

UNKNOWN

### Invitation

What if there was a tree house within the space of internal awareness? A place to return in order to feel safe and held.

No matter what may be happening in the forest of your life, you can always return to the sanctuary of your tree house.

You will find you have all that you need.

### Mindful Tip

There are endless ways to adapt this meditation by changing the location of the tree house to somewhere more or less familiar. Let your imagination run free.

»

# PRACTICE 56

Begin by finding a comfortable posture and by bringing your attention to the breath. Take a few moments to let yourself arrive and allow the breath to draw you gently into internal awareness. Allow the gaze to soften, the eyes to close.

1. You find yourself in an enormous forest. There are trees as far as the eye can see in every direction. This is the largest and most beautiful forest you have ever seen. You are in your tree house high up in the canopy of the forest. You remember this place from before and immediately feel safe and at ease.

2. Looking around the tree house you notice that it has everything you might need: food, water, clothes, blankets, books, even your journal. As you gaze out over the trees you hear the forest teeming with life. Animals call out to each other, the breeze whooshes through the leaves, birds sing and dance in colourful circles overhead. Take five breaths here.

3. It is summer and the forest canopy is thick with greenery. Leaves, vines and vegetation consume the view in every direction. Everywhere you look there are hues of green and brown, and gazing off into the distance you notice a haze of blue light above the treeline. Take five breaths here.

4. Autumn comes. The leaves start to turn and suddenly your daily view of the forest becomes a symphony of rich, new colours. Purples, reds, deep yellows and oranges. Take five breaths here.

5. One day you awaken to dark skies, an eerie black that can only announce an incoming storm. Safely in your tree house you have a prime view of the lightning in the distance. You hear the cracks of thunder, the shearing screech of trees ripped apart by airborne electricity. Take five breaths here.

6. Next comes the rain. With monsoon-force it beats down on the leaves all around. A crescendo of droplets fills the air. Cleansing, clearing, washing everything away. Take five breaths here.

7. As the storm passes and peace returns to the forest, the air feels fresh. Night falls and the cloudless sky is adorned with endless stars. Once again you drift into sleep. Take five breaths here.

8. When you awaken, the first of the winter snow covers the forest. A deep blanket of soft icing adorns the landscape and turns every sunbeam into an explosion of colour. Up in the tree house you are warm, safe and well. The observer. A witness of the days.

9.  Before long, the snow melts and the spring announces itself with new life, new growth, new promise. Wild flowers break ground on the forest floor. The trees are alive once more with song. Take five breaths here.

10. One day you realise you have witnessed everything that the weather and the rhythm of the seasons has to offer. The tree house in the centre of the forest has kept you safe and well throughout.

11. Return to wakefulness in your own way.

Record your experience in your Mindfulness Journal and the answers to these questions: What was your reaction to the storm? How did you feel in the tree house? Where do you feel safest in your life?

If practising with others, take turns sharing your discoveries.

# 57 Hollow Body

We shape clay into a pot, but it is the emptiness inside that holds whatever we want.

LAO TZU

## Invitation

Is it possible to enjoy being all of yourself, at once?

## Mindful Tip

As you become familiar with this visualisation, in moments of stress you will be able to take three colourful breaths and connect with the full resource of your awareness.

# PRACTICE 57

Begin by finding a comfortable posture and by bringing your attention to the breath. Take a few moments to let yourself arrive and allow the breath to draw you gently into internal awareness. Allow the gaze to soften, the eyes to close.

1. Imagine that your body is hollow and that when you breathe, the air moves into the full hollow cavity of your body, all at once.

2. Visualise this happening and pay close attention to any sensations that you notice, firstly in your abdomen. Take five breaths here.

3. Now visualise air moving through the arms, hands and fingers. Feel the feelings, sense the sensations, travel into the body on this flow. Take five breaths here.

4. Keeping the focus on the upper limbs, notice the downward flow of air on the inhalation and the upward flow on the exhalation. Take a further five breaths here.

5. Now take the focus of your awareness to your legs, feet and toes. Explore in the same way. Inhale air all the way down to the toes. Exhale all the way back to the nostrils and out. Take five breaths here.

6. On the next breath breathe into the head, the skull, the jaw, the eyes, the brain, the ears, the nose and mouth. Notice the specifics of the sensations that arise. Take your time to explore and take at least five breaths here.

7. Now breathe into the full body at once. Imagine that each breath completely fills the body and every exhalation cleanses the body.

8. Feel what it feels like to be all of your body at once. Take five breaths here.

9. Now, choose a relaxing colour and imagine it moving on the breath into the body.

10. Breathe your colour into your hollow body and observe the body's response. Take five breaths here.

11. Return to wakefulness in your own way.

Record your experience in your Mindfulness Journal noting the colour that you chose and its impact on your awareness.

If practising with others, take turns sharing your discoveries.

# 58 Compass Meditation

Two roads diverged in a wood,
and I, I took the one less travelled by,
And that has made all the difference.

ROBERT FROST

## Invitation

This meditation is not linked to the geographic directions
of the Earth but to the four corners of your awareness.
Allow each direction to have a voice.

## Mindful Tip

Develop this practice by standing and physically facing
North, East, South and West whilst working through the
instructions. If you are not sure which way is North, use
the four walls of any room to symbolise the compass points.

# PRACTICE 58

This is a spoken meditation. Choose whether to speak out loud or silently within internal awareness.

Begin by finding a comfortable posture and by bringing your attention to the breath. Take a few moments to let yourself arrive and allow the breath to draw you gently into internal awareness. Allow the gaze to soften, the eyes to close.

1. Allow your voice to complete each sentence stem by simply saying the three things that come to mind.

2. Welcome the stream of consciousness. Disengage your thinking mind. Invite your deepest wisdom to speak.

3. Turn now to the Northernmost point in the space of your awareness. Deepen your embrace of all that is North. Breathe the energy of North deep into every cell of your body. Take five breaths here.

4. Silently choose three words that represent your North and complete the following prompt. Do not worry if the words make no literal sense.

   *I am North, I am my … my … and my …*
   *Example: I am North, I am my **truth**, my **breath** and my **life**.*

5. Turn next to the Southernmost point in the space of your awareness. Deepen your embrace of all that is South. Breathe the energy of South deep into every cell of your body. Take five breaths here.

6. Silently choose three words that represent your South and complete the following prompt.

   *I am South, I am my … my … and my …*
   *Example: I am South, I am my **love**, my **compassion** and my **desire**.*

7. Turn next to the Easternmost point in the space of your awareness. Deepen your embrace of all that is East. Breathe the energy of East deep into every cell of your body. Take five breaths here.

8. Silently choose three words that represent your East and complete the following prompt.

   *I am East, I am my … my … and my …*
   *Example: I am East, I am my **arising**, my **creation** and my **dawn**.*

9. Turn next to the Westernmost point in the space of your awareness. Deepen your embrace of all that is West. Breathe the energy of West deep into every cell of your body. Take five breaths here.

»

10. Silently choose three words that represent your West and complete the following prompt.

   *I am West, I am my ... my ...*
   *and my ...*
   *Example: I am West, I am my* **peace,** *my* **reflection** *and my* **rest**.

11. Return to wakefulness in your own way.

Record any key words or sentences that came through in this practice in your Mindfulness Journal.

If practising with others, take turns sharing your discoveries.

# Mindfulness with Children

# 59 Smileyfulness

Sometimes your joy is the source of your smile, but sometimes your smile can be the source of your joy.

THICH NHAT HANH

## Invitation

This is a fun and simple visualisation that most children will enjoy. Before the exercise, read them the quote and ask them what they think it means.

## Mindful Tip

After the practice, invite the children to draw a picture of their smileyfulness meditation experience.

# PRACTICE 59

Settle into your seat and listen to the sounds of breathing. Close your eyes and relax. Calm and quiet. Breathing in, breathing out.

1. As you settle, imagine your head is filling up with tiny smiley faces, each beaming with happiness and bringing joyfulness to every part of your body! Can you feel the corners of your mouth rising into a little smile? Take five smiley breaths here.

2. Now imagine there are so many smiley faces in your head that there is no more room so they start dancing down into your arms, into your chest and into your belly. As they dance inside of you notice what you feel. Notice what you see. Take five happy breaths here.

3. Now there are so many smileys they are dancing down into your legs, feet and even your toes! Follow them through the body and feel what you feel.

4. Now take a deep breath into your body full of smiley faces! With every breath: more smiles, more joy, more happiness. Take five joyful breaths here.

5. Now listen, the smiley faces have a message just for you! Listen very carefully!

6. Now it is time to thank the smiley faces for visiting and wish them happiness on their journey. It is time to say goodbye.

7. Return to wakefulness in your own way.

Encourage the children to share their experiences.

# 60 Yes Unna

Row, row, row your boat. Gently down the stream. Merrily, merrily, merrily, merrily, life is but a dream.

ALICE MUNRO

## Invitation

The aim of this exercise is to help children feel comfortable closing their eyes whilst developing their mindfulness awareness skills.

Do not worry too much about posture for children at the beginning, just let them sit comfortably on the floor or chair.

If sitting on a chair, the instruction *feet on floor, bums on seats* is a simple and memorable one to start with.

## Mindful Tip

It is hard not to sing the call-and-response but do not worry if you do not have a singing voice; rapping the words works just as well.

With younger children practise the whole thing with eyes open, adding the eyes-closed aspect when they are more familiar with the game.

# PRACTICE 60

For this practice you will need a bell or chime.

Start by sitting down with the Caller facing the others. This is a call-and-response counting exercise. During the call everyone has their eyes open and during the response everyone closes their eyes. Unna is pronounced: 'uh-nah'.

It goes like this:

1. Call: *One Unna Two Unna Three Unna Four Unna*

   Response: *One Unna Two Unna Three Unna Four Unna*

2. Call: *Low Unna High Unna Left Unna Right Unna*

   Response: *Low Unna High Unna Left Unna Right Unna*

3. Call: *This Unna That Unna Which Unna Where Unna*

   Response: *This Unna That Unna Which Unna Where Unna*

4. Call: *Who Unna You Unna Who Unna Me Unna*

   Response: *Who Unna You Unna Who Unna Me Unna*

5. Call: *Yes Unna Yo Unna Yo Unna Yes Unna*

   Response: *Yes Unna Yo Unna Yo Unna Yes Unna*

6. Now repeat instructions 1–5 twice more.

7. After the final response there will be a large sigh:

8. Call: *Aaaaahhhhhhhhhh*

   Response: *Aaaaahhhhhhhhhh*

9. Spoken by Caller:

   *And now to dream your silent dream,*
   *Close your eyes and go within,*
   *When all is done the bell will ring.*

10. After a few minutes the Caller will ring a bell to signal the end of the game.

Encourage the children to share their experiences through words, drawing or dance.

# 61 Waterfulness

## It's kind of fun to do the impossible.

WALT DISNEY

### Invitation

In Tibet one of the ways that children learn mindfulness is by walking in a circle carrying full bowls of water. Waterfulness turns this practice into a fun game!

### Mindful Tip

Develop the game by having three rounds, each with the same course but a different activity:

Round 1: Waterfulness
Round 2: Egg and spoon
Round 3: Book on the head

If the adults or older children want to take part, try a soup spoon full of water instead of a bowl.

# PRACTICE 61

This is an eyes open meditation game to build focus and concentration. It is best to do this one in the kitchen where the floors can be dried easily, or outside so as not to worry about spills!

1. Begin by designing a course for participants to manoeuvre around.

2. The course could be on flat ground marked by a set of chairs, trees or cones. Or, if you have more time and space you could create a complicated course with ramps, things to step over and other obstacles.

3. Each player begins with a bowl of water filled almost to the very top. (How full the bowl is can be adjusted for different ages).

4. The aim of the game is to walk around the course without spilling any water.

5. All players start at the same time at different points along the course.

6. Overtaking is not allowed. There are no prizes for speed: this is not a race!

7. Players are encouraged to be silent throughout.

8. Set a timer for the length of the game; e.g. 1–5 minutes. Choose an appropriate duration based on the ages of the players. This can be increased as concentration builds. Alternatively play a song, which will indicate the start and end of the game.

Encourage the children to share their experiences.

# 62 The Quiet Corner

Because when the world quiets to the sound of your own breathing, we all want the same things: comfort, love and a peaceful heart.

MITCH ALBOM

## Invitation

The Quiet Corner is a sanctuary, a place where children can retreat when they are finding it hard to feel calm or safe.

The intention behind this practice is for children to find their way to the corner when they need it and by doing so, learn how to regulate their moods, and build their own practice of quiet reflection.

## Mindful Tip

Adults might ask whether a child would like to spend some moments in the Quiet Corner but it should never be used as a punishment, or as a location for serious talks or telling-off.

If your child has chosen to retreat to the Quiet Corner, respect their call for silence.

## PRACTICE 62

1. Consider if your Quiet Corner is to be a place for both adults and children or children alone. Create the space together with everyone's input. Shared and equal ownership of the project is important.

2. Now choose the best location for the Quiet Corner. If possible let it be somewhere away from the busiest and noisiest areas of the house. Maybe somewhere with a view of nature and, if not, perhaps there is space for a plant or flowers.

3. Next, consider how to furnish the Quiet Corner. Does it need a sofa, beanbag, cushions, blankets, some art, items of cultural or personal significance?

4. The aim is to create a simple, calming space that is truly comfortable, peaceful and welcoming.

5. As this is a corner of quiet reflection, make this an 'unplugged' space with no technology allowed. Instead, the Quiet Corner might have a resident teddy bear, paper and pens for doodling, even a squeezy stress toy.

6. Explain to your children that the Quiet Corner is a place where they can go at any time (within reason) to calm down, relax and reflect.

Away from the Quiet Corner encourage your children to share their experiences.

# 63 Mindfulness Bedtime

We are such stuff
As dreams are made on; and our little life
Is rounded with a sleep.

WILLIAM SHAKESPEARE

## Invitation

This is a guided meditation for parents to read to children
at bedtime to help them have the most relaxing, refreshing
and wonderful night's sleep.

## Mindful Tip

As you read through this practice, listen for changes in your
child's breathing. As they relax and release into sleep,
your voice can slow and quieten.

# PRACTICE 63

1. Start by snuggling down and finding the most comfy position for sleep.

2. Allow the eyes to close and your body to sink a little deeper into the warmth of your bed.

3. Notice the rise and fall of your chest. Allow each breath to relax your body, to quieten your mind, to soothe your muscles.

4. Let the journey of today fade into the background.

5. Breathe into all of your body and imagine the air moving like a beautiful white light down into your eyes and nose, your chest and tummy, your arms and legs, your fingers and toes.

6. Each new breath brings calming energy, inviting every tiny part of your body to let go, just for today.

7. Breathe and notice the white light moving through your body, bringing calm and stillness and gentle quiet.

8. Allow the breath to hold you, to carry you. Ride the waves of your breath into deeper calm. Breathe. Breathe. Breathe.

9. Here you are, surrounded by love, letting go, sinking into peaceful rest. Ahhhh. All is calm. You are safe and well. Surrounded by love. All is calm. All is quiet. That's right. That's right.

10. Here you are, surrounded by love, letting go, sinking into peaceful rest. Ahhhh. All is calm. You are safe and well, surrounded by love. All is calm. All is calm.

11. Repeat any part of the guided meditation that you enjoy until your child's breathing deepens and they fall asleep.

Now, the hard part: tip-toe away!

# 64 Rainbow Meditation

## Try to be a rainbow in someone's cloud.

MAYA ANGELOU

### Invitation

This is a calming and creative visualisation that helps children engage their inner vision and imagination.

### Mindful Tip

This practice can also be used as a bedtime meditation.

Shorten or lengthen the practice by doing more or less colours as you wish.

## PRACTICE 64

Allow all the children to find a comfortable seat or lie down. Then say:

1. Allow your eyes to gently close.

2. See if you can hear the quiet sounds of your breathing.

3. See if you can feel the little movements of your chest going up and down.

4. This is a rainbow meditation about the biggest, most beautiful rainbow in all of the World. There it is, ahead of you, stretching from one green hill to another. Take five breaths here and watch how the rainbow glows with all of its lovely colours.

5. This rainbow would love to share its colours with you. The first is the colour red.

6. So breathe red into your body. Let all your breaths be red. Let all your bones be red. Let all your thoughts be red thoughts. Let all your smiles be red.

7. What do you see inside? Where does red go? What does red do? How does red feel? What does red say? Listen. Take five breaths here.

8. The rainbow wants to share another colour with you. This colour is orange.

9. So breathe orange into your body. Let all your breaths be orange. Let all your bones be orange. Let all your thoughts be orange thoughts. Let all your smiles be orange.

10. What do you see inside? Where does orange go? What does orange do? How does orange feel? What does orange say? Listen. Take five breaths here.

11. Repeat instructions 8–10 for Yellow, Green, Blue, and Purple.

12. It is almost time to leave the rainbow and say goodbye to the colours.

13. Breathe gently as you slowly open your eyes.

Encourage the children to share their experiences through words, drawing or dance

# 65 Connecting with Babies

## We meet ourselves time and time again in a thousand disguises on the path of life.

CARL JUNG

### Invitation

Holding a baby is like holding the Universe in your arms. No wonder so many find it terrifying! Here is a simple process for connecting meaningfully with a baby, which also serves as a beautiful mindfulness practice for you.

### Mindful Tip

Imagine if we all intended to see, welcome and love each other on life's journey in this way.

## PRACTICE 65

1. Receive the baby with loving arms.

2. Allow your body to relax and soften.

3. Make gentle eye contact with the baby and take five breaths here.

4. Do not worry if the baby is initially distressed or becomes distressed at any point. Breathe consciously with an intention to be centred, calm and still in your own body. Breathe here for as long as it takes for the baby to reflect your calm.

5. Maintaining direct eye contact and keeping breathing calmly, silently repeat to the baby:

   *I see you.*
   *I welcome you.*
   *I love you.*

Record your experience of this practice in your Mindfulness Journal.

# 66 Mindfulness Rave

## Dance is the breath made visible.

ANNA HALPRIN

### Invitation

This practice contrasts our most active physical state with our quietest internal one.

### Mindful Tip

Turn this practice into a party game by having a referee who can call people out if they are moving during the silence.

# PRACTICE 66

This is a really fun mindfulness game for all ages. There is a dancing aspect and a sitting aspect. It is possible to play alone but it works best in a group of two or more. You will need music, a space to dance and somewhere to sit. If playing this at a children's party, an adult might demonstrate first so that everyone gets the idea.

1. Choose a really fun high-energy song that is guaranteed to get everyone involved dancing. Press play.

2. Dance your heart out. Go crazy. Big moves. Throw your shapes, let it all hang out!

3. Whoever is controlling the music will randomly press pause.

4. When the music stops everyone drops into their meditation sitting position and aims to immediately become still, tranquil and peaceful.

5. Whoever is controlling the music will randomly press play.

6. Everyone jumps up and goes crazy to the song and the game continues until everyone is exhausted.

When you have caught your breath, take turns sharing your experience.

In your Mindfulness Journal record how easy or difficult it was to shift from high energy dancing to stillness.

# Mindfulness for Creativity

# 67 The Creative Spark

## I never came upon any of my discoveries through the process of rational thinking.

ALBERT EINSTEIN

### Invitation

Remember, you are not only creative, you are creation, and the Creative Spark lights every move you make.

### Mindful Tip

This practice welcomes the experience of the unseen energy of creation that powers every cell in your body. This is the *chi* or *prana* spoken of in many of the wisdom traditions. It is your life force and your birthright.

# PRACTICE 67

Begin by finding a comfortable posture and by bringing your attention to the breath. Take a few moments to let yourself arrive and allow the breath to draw you gently into internal awareness. Allow the gaze to soften, the eyes to close.

1. Contemplate your body and the energy of life that is moving through it in this moment now. Take five breaths as you drop into this awareness.

2. Imagine that as you are breathing, life is breathing you. Play with this idea and take five breaths here.

3. On the next breath consider that your physical body, the you in which you reside, began as a single cell, which then divided and divided and created everything that you experience yourself to be.

4. Acknowledge the energy of creation in your body and take five breaths here.

5. Now, let go of the awareness of your body and bring your focus to the feelings of pure life force energy.

6. Notice any sensations, images, feelings and thoughts that arise and take five breaths here.

7. Next imagine that you can follow this creative energy of life itself through time and space to the beginning of all things; imagine that you can see the Creative Spark itself.

8. Take ten breaths here as the Creative Spark is revealed. Breathe. Watch. Listen.

9. Silently choose three words to describe what you see.

10. Take five breaths here.

11. Return to wakefulness in your own way.

Record your chosen words and reflections from this practice in your Mindfulness Journal.

If practising with others, take turns sharing your discoveries.

# 68 The Waterfall of Creativity

Chance is always powerful. Let your hook be always cast; in the pool where you least expect it, there will be a fish.

OVID

## Invitation

The energy of creativity is non-linear, spontaneous and multi-dimensional so disengage the analytical mind and allow the spirit of play to lead you into your creative nature.

## Mindful Tip

Having noted all of the gifts from the Waterfall of Creativity find out what they mean using one of the following continuation practices found overleaf.

# PRACTICE 68

Begin by finding a comfortable posture and by bringing your attention to the breath. Take a few moments to let yourself arrive and allow the breath to draw you gently into internal awareness. Allow the gaze to soften, the eyes to close.

1. Breathe in the warm air and notice the sounds of tropical birds in the distance. You find yourself walking along a sandy path. You are with a trusted guide and are feeling safe and supported. This is a trek to the fabled Waterfall of Creativity.

2. The day is warm and close and as the path winds deeper into the rainforest your excitement is growing. This is the very first time you have been invited on this journey.

3. People say you can ask the Waterfall of Creativity any question and answers will appear in the form of objects over the waterfall. You take five breaths here as you acknowledge your own questions.

4. Walking further into the rainforest, you round a corner and see the Waterfall of Creativity. Shimmering blue silvery water tumbles gracefully down from the river above into the deep lake. Take five breaths here.

5. Your fellow trekkers disperse along the shore and now alone, you find a grassy bank and sit at the edge of the crystal clear lake. You become quiet and still as the Waterfall of Creativity invites you to offer your first question in peaceful contemplation.

6. A question appears effortlessly and you sit with it resonating in your heart as you watch the flow of water. Take five breaths here as the Waterfall of Creativity responds.

7. As each object tumbles down into the lake, you gather all of the offerings and place them beside you on the bank. For now, you do not question for meaning, content to wait, witness, gather and breathe.

8. If you have further questions hold them in quiet contemplation in turn and the Waterfall will respond. Take as long as you need.

9. When your process is complete, give thanks to the Waterfall of Creativity for today's bounty. Take five breaths here.

10. Finally, pack up your objects into your bag and silently you journey home reflecting on the day.

11. Return to wakefulness in your own way.

Note the gifts you received in your Mindfulness Journal and reflect upon their meaning as suggested in the Mindful Tip.

If practising with others, take turns sharing your discoveries.

»

# CONTINUATION PRACTICES

Imagine that one of the gifts was a
blue fire engine.

## Solo practice - Write it

Take a pen and a blank sheet of paper
and for each gift complete the
following sentence.

The blue fire engine symbolises ...

Your aim is to fill a whole side with
writing in one minute. This means there
is no time to think, so let the words spill
out.
Do not worry if they come out in a
jumble of nonsense. Welcome
everything that comes.

Now read it back to see if a deeper
message has been revealed.

## Group practice - Speak it

If A saw the blue fire engine then B
will ask A:

*What does the blue fire engine
symbolise?*

A then answers for one minute,
without stopping.

During A's answer, B listens closely
without interrupting and then reflects
back what they have understood.

A discussion can then evolve naturally
from this starting point as you sense if a
deeper message is being revealed.

When ready, swap roles.

# 69 Meeting the Oracle

## Oh the places we'll go.

DR SEUSS

## Invitation

In this meditation you will meet The Oracle. The Oracle knows everything about all things, all people, backwards and forwards through time and space.

What questions will you take to The Oracle?

## Mindful Tip

Before doing this practice have a go at Practice 24, The Knowing Mind.

This practice can also be done in pairs with A asking the question and B speaking as The Oracle.

»

# PRACTICE 69

This is a mindfulness game, which engages the imagination and inner wisdom, here personified as The Oracle. You are going to ask your questions and also play the role of The Oracle.

Begin by finding a comfortable posture and by bringing your attention to the breath. Take a few moments to let yourself arrive and allow the breath to draw you gently into internal awareness. Allow the gaze to soften, the eyes to close.

1. Breathe in awareness of this moment and invite your playfulness to join you on this journey. Take five breaths here.

2. Locate your sense of curiosity and give yourself full permission to be silly.

3. Start by saying out loud:

   *I am ready to meet The Oracle.*

4. Now respond as The Oracle by greeting yourself in any way you choose.

   *The Oracle Speaks: ...*

5. Next say:

   *I have a question and I would be very grateful for your wisdom and guidance, great Oracle.*

6. Wait and see if The Oracle welcomes your question.

   *The Oracle Speaks: ...*

7. Now ask your question.

8. Before you respond as The Oracle, pause and breathe into your knowing. Give yourself full permission to access wisdom, foresight, intuition and creativity. When ready, answer in any way you wish.

   *The Oracle Speaks: ...*

9. Continue the conversation with further questions and answers until your practice feels complete.

10. Return to wakefulness in your own way.

In your Mindfulness Journal record anything that came through that feels important, true, or intriguing.

If practising with others, take turns sharing your discoveries.

# 70 The Doodle-Lution

## You cannot use up creativity. The more you use, the more you have.

MAYA ANGELOU

### Invitation

The mindful heart speaks a language of symbols, images and metaphors. Drop your words, and listen.

### Mindful Tip

When it is your turn to doodle, allow the lines to flow freely, automatically, aimlessly and spontaneously.

Welcome weird shapes, surprising shades and mysterious objects, let it all flow out.

»

# PRACTICE 70

This is an eyes-open mindfulness exercise to do with two or three people. You will need some paper and something to draw with.

1. It is not necessary to know at the beginning of the practice what the picture will be about, but if you do wish to have a focus for the doodle, choose a question, word or other prompt.

2. If using a focus or prompt, write it down on a separate piece of paper and turn it over. Let the focus now fade into the background and the doodle emerge organically without over-thinking.

3. The first person begins with a fresh sheet of paper and starts doodling.

4. After 30 seconds, pass the paper on to the next person.

5. The process continues with everyone taking turns. Watch as the doodle becomes what it wants to become.

6. Do not worry if someone draws over your shape, changes your lines, or creates something that does not seem to fit with your vision. Trust in the collaboration; something is emerging.

7. When the doodle is finished, it will tell you. Listen carefully. You will know when it is complete.

8. Now, if there was a focus, turn that sheet of paper back over and lay it side by side with the finished doodle.

9. Spend a few moments in contemplation of your joint creation and then take turns completing these sentences out loud.

   - *In this doodle I see ...*
   - *This doodle is showing me ...*

10. End with a free discussion of any further points that arise.

Record your sentences in your Mindfulness Journal.

# 71 The Mindful Story

## Unfold your own myth.

RUMI

## Invitation

Human stories have unexpected twists and turns. In this practice the aim is to go on a journey limited only by the elasticity of your imagination. No one person has ultimate control of where the story goes. This tale will be a creation of the group mind.

## Mindful Tip

Develop this practice by repeating it with these variations:

### Variation 1 - Holding hands

Follow the same practice but this time all hold hands in the circle. Does anything change?

### Variation 2 - Breathing together

Before unfolding your next myth, spend a few moments consciously breathing together. What do you notice about the story now?

»

# PRACTICE 71

This is a fun eyes-open mindfulness exercise to do in a group of two or more.

1. Gather seated in a circle.

2. Take a moment to look around. Make eye contact with your fellow storytellers and gently acknowledge one another.

3. The story commences with a single sentence from whoever wishes to begin.

   *Example: Once upon a time in a land far, far away lived a boy named Ocean ...*

4. The next person in the circle continues the story in any way they wish:

   *Example: Ocean lived with his parents, two sisters and his pet frog in a house made of seaweed ...*

5. The process continues around the circle with each subsequent person adding the next building block of the story. No need to think too hard about your contribution, let the story flow spontaneously.

6. Allow the story to develop and build. Useful prompts include:

   *And then ...*
   *Because of that ...*
   *Unexpectedly ...*

7. When the story reaches a conclusion, let the ending emerge naturally.

8. If the story was cut short, begin a new one!

Now take turns sharing what you noticed and learned through this story.

# 72 Dancing with the Muse

The Muse visits during the process of creation, not before. Do not wait for her. Start alone.

ROGER EBERT

## Invitation

Dance connects the human form with creativity and joy.

## Mindful Tip

If there is no art or photography on the walls or around your space, dance with your reflection in the windows or a mirror instead.

»

# PRACTICE 72

This is a moving meditation that begins in a standing position with eyes open. Make sure there is enough room to move safely around without bumping into anything.

Choose an up-beat piece of dance music that you love and press play.

1. Breathe, listen and dance!

2. As you move around the space and start throwing some shapes, dance on over to the first artwork or photograph that catches your eye.

3. Keep dancing and watch how your moving image is reflecting in the artwork or glass. Notice also the play of light and shadow in the room as you travel through the space.

4. Groove here until your curiosity moves you on.

5. Follow your dancing feet to another artwork and dance your heart out watching yourself and the image combine on the surface.

6. Repeat the process for as many images that you are drawn to, until the song comes to a close.

7. Breathe. Come back and sit in stillness.

8. Make space to see, hear and know any thoughts, ideas and solutions that are bubbling up in your awareness.

9. As you rest, gather your insights.

Record your insights in your Mindfulness Journal.

If practising with others, take turns sharing your discoveries.

# 73 The Engine of Serendipity

## The most beautiful thing we can experience is the mystery.

ALBERT EINSTEIN

### Invitation

Serendipity is the unfolding of events in an unexpectedly fortunate and beneficial way.

Opening to serendipity means opening to life.

You are the Engine of Serendipity.

### Mindful Tip

Serendipity arises when listening is present. Serendipity cannot arise when listening is absent.

»

## PRACTICE 73

Begin by finding a comfortable posture and by bringing your attention to the breath. Take a few moments to let yourself arrive and allow the breath to draw you gently into internal awareness. Allow the gaze to soften, the eyes to close.

1. Breathe deeply and allow your awareness to focus on the dark in front of your closed eyes. With each new breath notice the movement of light and darkness, and the changing colours. Take five breaths here.

2. The two-dimensional darkness transforms now into three-dimensional space and begins to form an unknown structure. Take five breaths here.

3. Allow your curiosity to explore the structure. Notice the lines, angles, colours and connections. This is the Engine of Serendipity. Take five breaths here.

4. You find yourself now inside the Engine of Serendipity. A unique machine: organic, beautiful, colourful. Take five breaths here.

5. Exploring further you see that the structure is made up of twists, turns, times, beginnings, ends and tunnels in between. Take five breaths here.

6. Some of the structure is solid, some fluid and some made of substances, the like of which you have never seen.

7. The solid areas of the structure move as you contemplate them. The liquid structures defy gravity. The shapes are almost too beautiful to be real. Take five breaths here.

8. Your heart races with excitement as you travel through, over, between and around the Engine of Serendipity.

9. As you listen closely, the sounds of the engine translate into a message. Take five breaths here.

10. Letting go of the need to make sense of your experience, merge with the Engine of Serendipity. Take five breaths here and notice what sensations, images, feelings and thoughts arise.

11. Ask yourself:

    *To what degree am I in tune with the Engine of Serendipity?*

    *To what degree am I in tune with the energy of life?*

12. Listen, and only when ready, return to the simplicity of the eyes-closed darkness and allow the Engine of Serendipity to fade into the background.

13. Return to wakefulness in your own way.

Record what you noticed about the
Engine of Serendipity in your
Mindfulness Journal.

If practising with others, take turns
sharing your discoveries.

# Fun Mindfulness Activities

# 74 Nature Meditation

## Adopt the pace of nature: her secret is patience.

RALPH WALDO EMERSON

## Invitation

There are few things in the modern world that hold the energy of profoundly authentic truth. Nature is one of them, which is why it is so precious to us and so deeply healing to human consciousness.

## Mindful Tip

If there is no easy access to a place of natural beauty nearby then do this exercise with your eyes closed by simply recalling somewhere stunning that you have been before.

## PRACTICE 74

This is an eyes-open meditation best done outdoors in a natural setting that inspires you. Your garden, the park, a nearby lake or forest: somewhere where you feel content and safe sitting quietly for a little while.

Begin by finding a comfortable posture and by bringing your attention to the breath. Take a few moments to let yourself arrive and allow the breath to draw you gently into internal awareness.

1.  Meet the natural world with the simplicity of this breath and call yourself into deep presence. Take five breaths here.

2.  Notice that your body is just as natural as the glorious nature that surrounds you. Take five breaths here.

3.  Look around slowly and pay attention to anything which calls your attention or arouses your curiosity.

4.  *What can you see that is alive?*

    Take five breaths here.

5.  *What can you hear that is alive?*

    Take five breaths here.

6.  *What can you smell that is alive?*

    Take five breaths here.

7.  *What do you feel that is alive?*

    Take five breaths here.

8.  Continue breathing and notice how you are connected to this place.

9.  Allow the division between you and what you are seeing to slip away.

10. Become part of the scene.

11. Breathe into and out of the life that surrounds you.

12. Listen.

13. Breathe.

14. Listen.

15. Return to wakefulness in your own way.

Describe carefully your experience of aliveness in your Mindfulness Journal.

If practising with others, take turns sharing your discoveries.

# 75 Mindfulness of Clouds

## It's not what you look at that matters, it's what you see.

HENRY DAVID THOREAU

### Invitation

Clouds are in a state of continual flow. They teach how to be fearless, how to embrace change, how to fly and how to disappear.

### Mindful Tip

With any eyes-open practice, the aim is to hold your focus on your internal state whilst also engaging fully with what you see. Experiment with this, trying to sense both your meditative internal awareness and your visual observations, simultaneously.

# PRACTICE 75

This is an eyes-open mindfulness practice. Pick somewhere quiet to sit with a clear view of the sky and the clouds and your Mindfulness Journal close by.

Begin by finding a comfortable posture and by bringing your attention to the breath. Take a few moments to let yourself arrive and allow the breath to draw you gently into internal awareness.

1. Watch the sky and allow your curiosity to direct your attention to a single cloud. Watch for light, colours, mood and motion. Take five breaths here.

2. Consider these questions:

   *What is the cloud made of?*
   *What am I made of?*

3. Take five breaths here.

4. Follow the cloud as it changes. Really observe it. See if you can notice every bend, twist, shift and flow. Breathe here and contemplate the aspects of your body that are also in motion. Take five breaths here.

5. Observe the journey of the cloud across the sky and consider these questions:

   *Is it alone or travelling in a procession?*
   *Where did it come from?*
   *Where was it created?*
   *Where is it going?*

6. Take five breaths here.

7. Now ask yourself:

   *Where did I come from?*
   *Where am I going?*

8. Take five breaths here.

9. Allow your curiosity to take your focus deeper into the cloud and ask:

   *What is your purpose?*

10. Listen deeply and take five breaths here.

11. Breathe and then consider the question:

    *What is my purpose?*

12. Take five breaths here.

13. Next, allow your curiosity to draw your attention to another cloud. Tune into the rhythm of this cloud's motion by observing it closely.

14. As you pay attention to the gentle transitions occurring within the cloud, imagine these are linked to the rhythm of your breath. Breathe with the cloud.

15. Stay connected to the cloud until your practice feels complete.

16. Return to wakefulness in your own way.

»

Now record your answers in your
Mindfulness Journal.

If practising with others, take turns
sharing your discoveries.

# 76 Tree Meditation

## Why not go out on a limb?
## That's where the fruit is.

WILL ROGERS

### Invitation

Trees hold wisdom, and will release it generously
in the company of quiet contemplation.

### Mindful Tip

This exercise is described as a visualisation but also works
beautifully outside in a forest you know well. If the forest
is unfamiliar, take care so you do not actually get lost!

»

# PRACTICE 76

Begin by finding a comfortable posture and by bringing your attention to the breath. Take a few moments to let yourself arrive and allow the breath to draw you gently into internal awareness. Allow the gaze to soften, the eyes to close.

1. You find yourself in an enormous forest. Although you seem to be lost, you feel safe, happy and confident. You look around, stunned by the beauty of this moment. You notice the play of light swirling through the branches, the sounds of leaves shimmering all around.

2. Continuing onwards, a tiredness comes over you, unlike anything you have felt before. You try to resist, but your vision is becoming hazy and your steps now seem less sure. It feels like the ground itself is soft and moving.

3. Sensing you must rest, you walk onwards following a subtle pull that is leading you deeper into the forest. You are being called somewhere, by something. Although disoriented, you still have a sure sense that everything is OK and that you are being taken care of.

4. Now, well off the forest trail you find yourself slowly walking, almost stumbling through the undergrowth, the closely-knit trees and bushes pushing you down trails previously only travelled by the forest animals.

5. The subtle pull that is compelling you forward strengthens suddenly. Looking up a magnificent tree is welcoming you under its broad branches.

6. Relieved to have found a place to rest you nestle into the base of the tree and find that your body fits perfectly into the tree trunk as if it had been designed to hold you. Take five breaths here.

7. Relax here, your breath releases into a depth and clarity rarely experienced.

8. The mind releases too and becomes overwhelmed by the flow of love moving into your body from the tree.

9. You have never been held in quite this way. Take five breaths here.

10. Give yourself to this experience, trusting and knowing that the tree is always available for you and that you have full permission to journey back here at any time.

11. When ready, ask the tree if it has a message for you. Take five breaths here and listen openly.

12. If you have a message for the tree, offer it now.

13. Rest here for as long as you wish, and if a conversation arises between you and the tree, participate fully.

14. When the experience feels complete, gently find your way home.

15. Return to wakefulness in your own way.

Record any messages that were exchanged in your Mindfulness Journal.

If practising with others, take turns sharing your discoveries.

# 77 Mindfully Eating (Chocolate)

## All you need is love. But a little chocolate now and then does not hurt.

CHARLES M SCHULZ

## Invitation

Becoming more mindful about the physical experience of eating is the first step in becoming more mindful about eating habits.

If your aim is to become more conscious about food choices, when considering what to eat, test the options by sensing why your body is calling for this food. Listen particularly to the body's genuine call for nourishment and learn to distinguish other drivers such as addiction and greed. Bringing increased body awareness to your motivations around food will serve you well if you are being intentional in the creation of your body.

With practice and by increasing compassion and limiting the impulse to judge, it is possible to navigate food choices more mindfully and offer the body the authentic nourishment that it seeks.

## Mindful Tip

The most common mindful eating practice uses a raisin, which is a lot less messy than chocolate, which tends to melt in the palm. However, Mr Schulz makes a good point. Everything is better with chocolate!

You can of course try this one with any type of food: jelly babies, gummy bears, m&m's, apples and carrots all work well, so feel free to mix things up.

How about trying this practice with your sandwich at lunch today?

# PRACTICE 77

Begin by finding a comfortable posture and by bringing your attention to the breath. Take a few moments to let yourself arrive and allow the breath to draw you gently into internal awareness.

1. Pick up the square of chocolate with finger and thumb and place it on your palm.

2. As you do so, notice what thoughts and feelings are arising within as you bring your attention to this object. Take five breaths here.

3. With one finger, touch the chocolate. What does it actually feel like. Be precise and detailed in your exploration. Take five breaths here exploring the tactile sensations.

4. If the chocolate is starting to melt on your palm notice the feelings associated with that. Be specific in your observations. Take five breaths here.

5. Smell the chocolate as if you had never done so before. Silently choose three words to describe what you sense and do not worry if your words are abstract associations. Let the mind freewheel.

6. Now place the piece of chocolate on your tongue but resist the urge to bite or chew. Allow the gaze to soften and your eyes to close. Take five breaths here.

7. What happens in your mouth? What do you feel, sense, taste. Notice the arising of any desire to bite, chew or swallow and any others.

8. Next, take a single bite and divide the piece in two but still resist the urge to chew or take further bites. Take five breaths here.

9. Now, with full attention, slowly and carefully begin the chewing process. Consciously follow the movements of your tongue, teeth and jaw.

10. Notice the urge to swallow arising and again, just for now, resist it.

11. Only when it becomes impossible to chew the chocolate any more, allow yourself to swallow.

12. Finally, imagine following the chocolate on its path down into the body. Trace the tiny sensations of the swallow moving the chocolate down the throat and into the stomach. How long can you stay aware of its journey? Take five breaths here.

13. Repeat as desired.

14. Return to wakefulness in your own way.

In your Mindfulness Journal record how this experience was different from your everyday experience of eating.

If practising with others, take turns sharing your discoveries.

# 78 Measuring Subtle Energy

## Vision is the art of seeing what is invisible to others.

JONATHAN SWIFT

### Invitation

The aim of this fun game is to increase awareness of subtle energies by demonstrating, visibly and experientially, the energy field of the human body.

### Mindful Tip

Try this exercise at different times of the day to see what changes you can notice in the energy field.

# PRACTICE 78

You will need a reasonably large room and a piece of L-shaped wire. The corner of a metal hanger works perfectly. Take care and ensure adult supervision if you have to cut it. An approximate size for each side of the wire is 15–20 centimetres. Participants in this exercise will be referred to as A and B.

1. A stands at the end of the room facing B with arms by their sides.

2. B stands at the other end of the room holding the wire in one hand and facing A.

3. B holds the wire in their dominant hand with one end of the wire pointing down to the floor through the closed hand and one end pointing at A.

4. It is very important that the wire can move freely within B's hand and therefore B holds the wire somewhat loosely. Check the wire can move by giving it a little twirl and it should rotate freely.

5. B now sets an intention that the wire will turn to the side when it meets A's energy field.

6. With the wire pointing straight towards A, B now slowly approaches. Both participants watch for any movement of the wire. If B's focus and intention is clear, the wire will very obviously turn when B reaches the edge of A's energy field.

7. Do not be concerned if your field is larger or smaller than others. Your energy field fluctuates and is constantly changing.

8. Now swap positions and repeat the exercise.

9. If practising with more than 2 people, continue with C testing B and so on until everyone has had a go.

Record what you discover about your energy fields in your Mindfulness Journal.

Take turns sharing your experience.

# 79 Dancefulness

The body is living art. Your movement
through time and space is art.
A painter has brushes. You have your body.

ANNA HALPRIN

## Invitation

This exercise is not about dancing. It is about noticing
where movement comes from.

Feel for the impulse of movement that arises within,
generated in response to your emotions and the music.

Follow the movement from emotion to motion.

## Mindful Tip

To bring additional spontaneity to this exercise, select a
piece of music that is less familiar. It is easier to let go into
mindful movement when the body has not danced the
piece many times before.

When familiar with this practice, as you choose the piece
of music, set an intention for your dance by asking yourself:

*What am I dancing for?*

Your intention might be:

*I am dancing for peace.*
*I am dancing to heal my relationship with ...*
*I am dancing to express my ...*
*I am dancing to understand ...*

# PRACTICE 79

This is a moving meditation that begins in a standing position with eyes closed. Make sure there is enough room to move safely around without bumping into anything.

Select a piece of music and press play.

1. Listen to the music in stillness.

2. Wait.

3. Listen.

4. Begin to notice the very first impulse of movement arising in your body but for now resist it. Just notice the impulse arising.

5. Breathe.

6. Now, as the impulse builds, let the movement come.

7. Follow your body, your hands, your feet, your hips.

8. Find new shapes, new patterns, new ways of moving.

9. Follow the rhythm, the beat, the wave.

10. Let the impulses guide you throughout the piece until the music stops and you come back to rest in stillness.

11. Return to wakefulness in your own way.

Record your experience in your Mindfulness Journal. Note in particular any body sensations or movements that felt new.

If practising with others, take turns sharing your discoveries.

# 80 Mindfulness with Animals / Pets

Dogs do not see the outside of a human but the inside of a human.

CESAR MILAN

## Invitation

Pets are more than companions and healers; they are teachers too. My labrador Ty can always be counted on to remind me to be playful, loving and to relax.

*What is your pet teaching you?*

## Mindful Tip

Build your capacity for this type of contact gradually and do not expect huge revelations instantly.

Learning to connect in this way takes time and patience.

# PRACTICE 80

Begin by finding a comfortable posture and by bringing your attention to the breath. Take a few moments to let yourself arrive and allow the breath to draw you gently into internal awareness.

1. If your pet is with you begin by holding or stroking your pet and making gentle eye contact. Spend a few moments connecting and sensing your unique bond. Take five breaths here.

2. When you feel connected, allow the gaze to soften, the eyes to close.

3. If you are not currently with your pet physically, or if your pet has passed away, bring them to mind by picturing them and imagine the feeling of your pet being close. Take five breaths here.

4. Now, set a silent, strong intention to be one hundred per cent present with your pet. Take five breaths here.

5. Next, open your heart to your pet and imagine your pet's heart is opening also. Imagine, feel and visualise connecting heart to heart.

6. Send your pet a silent greeting. Listen. Take five breaths here.

7. Tell the pet anything you wish them to know at this time. Take five breaths here.

8. Ask the animal any questions that you wish and listen for a response whether it comes in words, images, emotions or simply a sense of knowing.

9. Conclude the connection with any final words, intentions or commitments that come.

10. Take five final breaths in gratitude for your pet.

11. Return to wakefulness in your own way.

In your Mindfulness Journal record your experience and any responses you felt, saw or heard, no matter how subtle.

If practising with others, take turns sharing your discoveries.

# 81 Best Thing / Worst Thing

## Everything has beauty, but not everyone can see.

CONFUCIUS

### Invitation

Best Thing/Worst Thing is a wonderfully simple game to play at any social gathering where there is a desire to nurture a sense of compassion, find out about each other's day, and increase self-awareness.

### Mindful Tip

Try this one at family mealtimes; it works well with all ages.

As each person reflects on their day, the group simply holds a space of welcoming, curiosity and love.

# PRACTICE 81

This is an eyes-open mindfulness game that can be played at any time with any group. In the description that follows it is described at a family mealtime.

1. Once the meal is served, ask for a volunteer to begin and then go around the table clockwise taking turns.

2. Each person reflects upon their day and chooses two things that happened to tell the group. One should be the Best Thing that happened and the other, the Worst Thing.

3. There are a few rules:

   i. Phones/laptops/tablets away.
   ii. The things must have happened today before you sat down for the meal.
   iii. Nobody is allowed to say:
   *The best thing is that we are all together.*
   iv. Whilst a player is taking their turn, a little encouragement is allowed for the little ones, but otherwise the group should listen attentively until they have finished before commenting.

4. Enjoy!

Part C

# ADVANCED PRACTICES

# Taking Mindfulness Further

# 82 Advanced Breathing

People are scared to empty their minds fearing they will be engulfed by the void. What they do not realise is that their own mind is the void.

HUANG-PO

## Invitation

Within these visualisations notice carefully the impact of each on your internal experience and be alive to your own intuitive response.

Just as these visualisations emerged from my own practice, new variations may reveal themselves within the space of yours.

## Mindful Tip

Take your time with this one. Stay with a stage until the visualisation is easy and comfortable before moving on.

Remember that the analytical mind will struggle as the visualisations become more complex, so allow your creative mind to see the patterns emerging as art, and let the breath show you the way.

# PRACTICE 82

Begin by finding a comfortable posture and by bringing your attention to the breath. Take a few moments to let yourself arrive and allow the breath to draw you gently into internal awareness. Allow the gaze to soften, the eyes to close.

## STAGE 1 - Drawing in light

1. Connect with the breath and visualise a white light travelling from the top of your head, into the heart and then out the soles of the feet into the core of the Earth.

2. Inhale down into the heart, exhale down into the Earth.

3. Repeat on each breath, paying close attention to how your physical body responds.

4. If the practice feels clear and stable move to the next stage.

## STAGE 2 - Drawing in light from two directions

1. Visualise the breath bringing white light in from above and in from below at the same time.

2. On the inhalation one beam of light moves down into the heart, through the body and out the perineum whilst another beam of light moves up through the body, into the heart and out the head. As the beams cross, watch and feel how they interact. Notice if they spiral, merge or pass by.

3. Repeat on each breath, paying close attention to how the physical body responds.

4. Practise this until the visualisation is easy and the sensations within the body are steady and comfortable.

## STAGE 3 - Breathing in light from four directions

1. Expand the Stage 2 visualisation with two more beams of light, one from your left and one from your right.

2. The two new beams enter the sides of your abdomen approximately at the bottom of the ribs. As each enters, it passes through your centre (where all four beams converge) before passing out the opposite side.

3. On each inhalation four beams of light move into the body converging in your centre. On each exhalation the beams pass through and out.

4. As the beams cross, watch and feel how they interact, noticing if they spiral, merge or simply pass by.

5. Repeat on each breath, paying close attention to how your physical body responds.

6. Practise this until the visualisation is easy and the sensations within the body are steady and comfortable.

»

## STAGE 4 - Spherical Breathing

1. The previous stages have all been in preparation for Spherical Breathing.

2. Imagine you are sitting inside a large sphere of light. On each inhalation draw the light from all around you into the centre of the body. On each exhalation the light moves through the centre in all directions and back into the sphere of light.

3. Inhale the light in all directions; exhale the light in all directions.

4. The light is now moving from all directions into the body and out of the body with every complete breath.

5. Pay close attention to how your physical body responds.

6. Practise this until the visualisation feels easy and the sensations within the body are steady and comfortable.

## Optional continuation

7. Practise Stage 4 Spherical Breathing for five minutes.

8. Contemplate a question or issue of your choice.

9. Listen.

## STAGE 5 - Infinity Spherical Breathing

1. In the final stage of this exercise the light is visualised moving both in and out of the centre at the same time.

2. On the inhalation draw light from the sphere into your centre as in Stage 4 whilst simultaneously moving light from your centre into the sphere.

3. On each exhalation the same thing occurs: light moves from the sphere to the centre and from the centre to the sphere.

4. Hold the intention and idea of the exercise loosely in your mind's eye and allow your artistic aspect to create the visual. Alternatively, feel the exchange occurring within the body and hold the knowing of this in your awareness.

5. As the vision takes shape, breathe deeply into and out of your centre, noting any sensations and associations that arise. Pay particular attention to your awareness of connection.

6. Practise Stage 5 until the visualisation is easy and the sensations within your body are steady and comfortable.

## Optional continuation

7.  Practise Stage 5 Infinity Spherical
    Breathing for five minutes.

8.  Contemplate a question or issue of
    your choice.

9.  Listen.

As you move through the stages,
record your discoveries in your
Mindfulness Journal.

If practising with others, take turns
sharing your experience.

# 83 Mindfulness of Decisions

## The major way to conquer fear is to make a decision.

RESHAD FIELD

## Invitation

Mindfulness informs decision-making by taking it from a purely mental experience into an embodied, full-being experience.

This practice allows you to test a potential decision against the body's inherent wisdom.

## Mindful Tip

If it feels uncomfortable when asking if the decision is kind, then consider whether you are taking care of yourself and others with this choice.

Is there a more compassionate approach that you might take?

Note that your decision need not be 'nice'. The kind thing to do might still be very challenging for someone affected by that decision.

# PRACTICE 83

Reflect on an issue or dilemma that needs a decision. Choose a solution to focus on and then follow the practice through.

Begin by finding a comfortable posture and by bringing your attention to the breath. Take a few moments to let yourself arrive and allow the breath to draw you gently into internal awareness. Allow the gaze to soften, the eyes to close.

1. Allow the breath to centre you and become present in this moment.

2. Call yourself into full awareness.

3. As you become still and quiet, bring the focus of your attention to the felt sensations within the body that arise in response to each question.

4. As you become accustomed to this practice, it will be your task to familiarise yourself with the body's responses.

5. As a guide, if the body feels open and relaxed and your energy is freely flowing, consider that a *yes*.

6. If you feel uneasiness, sadness, tightness or constraint in the body, that is a *no*.

7. Clarity in this practice comes from clear awareness of felt responses. The mind will be invited to return for analysis afterwards.

## QUESTION 1 – Is my decision clear?

8. Ask yourself the first question:

   *Is my decision clear?*

   Take at least five breaths as you tune into the body's responses, listening for sensations, images, feelings and words.

## QUESTION 2 – Is my decision stable?

9. Ask yourself the second question:

   *Is my decision stable?*

   Take at least five breaths as you tune into the body's responses, listening for sensations, images, feelings and words.

## QUESTION 3 – Is my decision true for me?

10. Ask yourself the third question:

    *Is my decision true for me?*

    Take at least five breaths as you tune into the body's responses, listening for sensations, images, feelings and words.

»

## QUESTION 4 – Is my decision wise?

11. Ask yourself the fourth question:

    *Is my decision wise?*

    Take at least five breaths as you tune into the body's responses, listening for sensations, images, feelings and words.

## QUESTION 5 – Is my decision kind?

12. Ask yourself the fifth question:

    *Is my decision kind?*

    Take at least five breaths as you tune into the body's responses, listening for sensations, images, feelings and words.

13. Now that you have recorded the very specific felt responses from the body, allow the mind to come back in for further analysis.

14. If you feel your decision has now changed, test the new decision in the same way by following the exercise through once more. Further repetitions are often much speedier than the first round.

15. Return to wakefulness in your own way.

Record the information that you gathered in your Mindfulness Journal.

If practising with others, take turns sharing your discoveries.

# 84 Candle Mindfulness

## Ask yourself: In the face of vulnerability, what do you bring?

GEORGINA EDEN

### Invitation

This is a deceptively simple practice in which there are many lessons, not least about vulnerability.

No human life is free of vulnerability, uncertainty or tragedy, but as my teacher Georgina Eden implies, there is always a choice as to what to bring in the face of it.

### Mindful Tip

Some questions to reflect on that arise from this practice:

*To what degree can I hold still, whilst the world around me is in motion?*

*What becomes possible when I retain my awareness of stillness, whilst relating to others?*

»

# PRACTICE 84

Set a timer for five or ten minutes.

Begin by finding a comfortable posture and by bringing your attention to the breath. Take a few moments to let yourself arrive and allow the breath to draw you gently into presence.

1. Light a candle and sit in front of it. Take five breaths here.

2. The candle is a symbol of impulse and change: your awareness, a symbol of the response.

3. Breathe and connect with the flame by observing it closely. Feel the movements of the flame, the rise and fall, the back and forth. Let it breathe with you. Take five breaths here.

4. Maintain your focus on the flame whilst now focussing equally on your inner experience. Take five breaths here.

5. Set an intention to remain internally still.

6. All of your awareness is with the flame. All of your awareness is with inner stillness. Breathe into the unity of both.

7. Continue the practice until the timer sounds.

8. Return to wakefulness in your own way.

In your Mindfulness Journal record any sensations, images, feelings and thoughts that arose during this meditation.

If practising with others, take turns sharing your discoveries.

# 85 Alignment

This is the real secret to life, to be completely engaged with what you are doing in the here and now, and instead of calling it work, realise it is play.

ALAN WATTS

## Invitation

Alignment feels quite different to success. Whilst success is predominantly ego-driven, alignment goes far deeper. Consequently, whilst the ego is never satisfied, no matter how many awards, prizes or bonuses are gathered, the gifts of alignment are peace, contentment and a distinct feeling of having, and more importantly being, enough.

Whilst success is easily lauded by others, alignment is a little quieter, and once you have it, you do not need others to tell you: well done.

## Mindful Tip

After this practice reflect on the following questions:

*Am I more or less aligned than I was 5 years ago?*

*How might I welcome more alignment into my life?*

»

# PRACTICE 85

Begin by finding a comfortable posture and by bringing your attention to the breath. Take a few moments to let yourself arrive and allow the breath to draw you gently into internal awareness. Allow the gaze to soften, the eyes to close.

1. Drop any and all current ideas of what you think alignment looks like and settle deeply into the breath, and this moment.

2. Give yourself full permission to access a new and more truthful experience of alignment. Take five breaths here.

3. Acknowledge the alignment that is held within every cell of your body. Take five breaths here.

4. Next, through the power of your intention, ask the body to show you what aligned breathing feels like. Trust the body and take five aligned breaths.

5. As you sit, ask the body to align itself and observe your posture change with large, small and microscopic adjustments. Take five breaths here.

6. Bring your awareness next to your thoughts and allow your deepest personal source of alignment to align the mind. Take five breaths here.

7. As you centre yourself in the energy of alignment, think back over the last 24 hours, and consider the degree to which your thoughts and words have resonated with the vibration of alignment.

8. Notice both alignments and misalignments without judging and be specific in your observations. Take five breaths here.

9. Centre yourself deeper in the energy of alignment, think back over the last 24 hours, and consider the degree to which your actions have resonated with the vibration of alignment.

10. Once again, notice both alignments and misalignments without judging and be specific in your observations. Take five breaths here.

11. Finally contemplate the question:

    *To what degree am I aligned in my life?*

12. Take five breaths here and listen.

13. Return to wakefulness in your own way.

Record your current experience of alignment in your Mindfulness Journal and consider the questions suggested in the Mindful Tip.

If practising with others, take turns sharing your discoveries.

# 86 Flower of Life

## Learn how to see. Realise that everything connects to everything else.

LEONARDO DA VINCI

### Invitation

The Flower of Life is a symbol found within many of the ancient wisdom traditions.

It is said to be the sacred geometric representation of life itself.

### Mindful Tip

As a variation to this practice swap the geometric image for a real flower and follow the instructions again.
What do you notice?

»

# PRACTICE 86

Begin by finding a comfortable posture and by bringing your attention to the breath. Take a few moments to let yourself arrive and allow the breath to draw you gently into internal awareness.

1. Turn to the image of the Flower of Life. Gaze upon it with the full presence of your awareness. Take five breaths here.

2. Each time a thought or some commentary arises in your mind, bring your awareness gently back to focus fully on the image once again.

3. Breathe here in steady contemplation. Lose yourself in the Flower. Take five breaths here.

4. Allow the focus of your eyes to soften slightly and notice what occurs.

5. Allow whatever comes to come. Take five breaths here.

6. Now allow the gaze to soften and the eyes to close. See if you can hold on to the image in your mind's eye. Take five breaths here.

7. Now let the focus on your internal image fade and follow whatever occurs within the space of your awareness. Take five breaths here.

8. Pay attention to all sensations, images, feelings and thoughts. Take five further breaths.

9. Stay with the practice until it feels complete.

10. Return to wakefulness in your own way.

Record what you noticed and felt in your Mindfulness Journal.

If practising with others, take turns sharing your discoveries.

# 87 Mindfulness of Pure Awareness

You are not merely the body;
you are 100% Pure Being. But you must
find this out for yourself. It must become
your own discovery, happening in your
innermost being.

MOOJI

## Invitation

As Mooji says, the discoveries that lie within mindfulness practice are personal. They will be found and experienced solely by you.

Whilst the instructions in this practice are deceptively simple, the practice is not. Rest assured the instructions will not lead you anywhere you are not ready to go.

## Mindful Tip

It is possible within this practice for the breath to slow and appear to almost stop. If this does occur, know that it is perfectly normal: there is nothing to be afraid of.

Allow yourself to experience this new depth of quiet within your being, and hold steady in the knowledge that the breath will return at exactly the right time.

## PRACTICE 87

Begin by finding a comfortable posture and by bringing your attention to the breath. Take a few moments to let yourself arrive and allow the breath to draw you gently into internal awareness. Allow the gaze to soften, the eyes to close.

1. Bring your focus inward. Take five breaths here.

2. Listen to what is arising. Take five further breaths here.

3. Invite the full experience of yourself to be welcome, seen and heard. Take at least five breaths here.

4. Continue breathing and let the specifics of that which is arising and your experience of it to fade gradually away. Something is happening.

5. As you become still and close with silence, notice that life is happening.

6. Breathe in spontaneous, living awareness.

7. Be.

8. Spend as long as you wish in this space.

9. Return to wakefulness in your own way.

Record your discoveries in your Mindfulness Journal.

If practising with others, take turns sharing your experiences.

# Mindfulness and Healing

# 88 Subtle Energy Awareness

There is a desire deep within the soul which drives man from the seen to the unseen, to philosophy and to the divine.

KAHLIL GIBRAN

## Invitation

I had a coaching client once who told me that he was not interested in energy healing as he did not believe in anything he could not see for himself.

I then asked him the following questions:

*Do you believe in electricity?*
*Do you believe in wifi?*
*Do you believe in magnets?*
*Do you believe in the radio?*
*Do you believe in your TV remote control?*

He laughed and booked in for a healing.

## Mindful Tip

This exercise can be developed by practising Advanced Breathing, as described in Practice 82, either before or during the practice. Notice if and how this changes what you experience and perceive.

# PRACTICE 88

This is an eyes-open exercise.

1. Rub the palms of your hands together quickly for about ten seconds then hold them about 10 centimetres apart.

2. Now focus on any tiny sensations that you can feel in your palms.

   *What do you experience?*

   Take five breaths here.

3. Rub the palms together again for ten seconds and then hold them 10 centimetres apart. This time let your hands come towards each other without touching and then apart, then closer and apart so that they are gently moving in and out. The motion is like a little bounce.

   *What do you feel?*

   Take five breaths here.

4. Once more, rub your palms together for ten seconds and then hold them 10 centimetres apart. Now play with the sensations by moving your hands in any way you choose. See how far you can pull your palms apart without losing the sensation of energy connection. Take five breaths here.

5. What happens when you pull one hand down and one hand up?

6. Rotate your palms. What do you notice?

7. Experiment further and gather experiential knowledge of how energy moves through your hands. Take five breaths here.

## Optional continuation

8. In pairs, now sit or stand facing each other. Each person rubs their own palms together and then with the left palm facing up and right palm down hold your hands 10cm above or below your partner's.

9. Repeat the exercise one more time to see if the sensations change or evolve.

Detail the physical sensations that you perceived in your Mindfulness Journal.

When both ready, share any sensations, images, feelings and thoughts that came up.

# 89 Healing White Light

There is not enough darkness
in all the World to snuff out the light
of one little candle.

GAUTAMA BUDDHA

## Invitation

Light and healing go together.

Allow the light of your awareness to guide you through this
gentle healing practice.

## Mindful Tip

Within your visualisation, notice where the light shines most
brightly as this is where it is needed most.

# PRACTICE 89

Begin by finding a comfortable posture and by bringing your attention to the breath. Take a few moments to let yourself arrive and allow the breath to draw you gently into internal awareness. Allow the gaze to soften, the eyes to close.

1. Settle in and notice the rhythm of your breath. Follow it. Observe it. Notice the smallest sensations of breathing. Track the breath through the nose, the airways, the lungs and the chest. Notice too the ripple of movement felt within the whole body as it follows the gentle wave of expansion and release. Take five breaths here.

2. On the next breath imagine breathing a healing white light into the body. This luminous substance comes from an infinite source and brings with it health, strength, vitality, peace, joy and rejuvenation. Imagine you are linked to this light and can draw from it now, and at any time. Take five breaths here.

3. Watch the white light move through the body in all directions. Take five breaths here.

4. Next, welcome the healing light into your lungs, chest and heart. Let it gather and swell. Take five breaths here.

5. On each inhale draw more light into the body. On each exhale feel tension and tightness being released. Take five breaths here.

6. Then, breathe the white light directly into the heart. Take five healing breaths here.

7. Now, notice the light moving up through the neck and into the head. The light brings its gift of healing. Notice what happens as you take five breaths here.

8. Next allow the light to move through the shoulders, arms, hands and fingers. Explore. How do those parts of your body respond? Take five breaths here.

9. Now, slowly allow the healing light to travel down into the abdomen, illuminating the hips, the thighs, the lower legs and into the feet and toes. What do you feel? Take five breaths here.

10. Finally, bring the awareness back to the heart and breathe peacefully.

11. What have you noticed in this practice?

12. Return to wakefulness in your own way.

Record your discoveries in your Mindfulness Journal.

If practising with others, take turns sharing your experience.

# 90 Self-Healing

## The wound is the place where the Light enters you.

RUMI

### Invitation

Healing means: opening to life, dissolving fear,
and letting go.

### Mindful Tip

Familiarise yourself with Practices 88 and 89 before
trying this one.

# PRACTICE 90

Lie down for this exercise but take care to remain aware and alert. If you do fall asleep, do not worry but you might want to set an alarm just in case.

Begin by finding a comfortable posture and by bringing your attention to the breath. Take a few moments to let yourself arrive and allow the breath to draw you gently into internal awareness. Allow the gaze to soften, the eyes to close.

1. Rub the palms of your hands together quickly for about 30 seconds to commence the flow of energy. Imagine that your breath is connected to an infinite source of healing white light infused with love, rejuvenation, joy and vitality.

2. As you breathe in, imagine the white light is flowing into the heart and as you breathe out, imagine the white light is passing down your arms and out of the palms of your hands.

3. During each hand position you will need to keep this visualisation in mind as it catalyses the flow of energy.

4. In each of the hand positions use a slightly cupped hand rather than a flat palm.

5. Begin by bringing your hands down gently over your eyes. Do not press down but softly rest your cupped hands on your skin with the centre of your palm above the eyes. No part of your hand should touch your eyelids.

6. Notice any sensations, images, feeling and thoughts that arise in your awareness and stay in this hand position for about twenty breaths.

7. Next, bring your cupped palms to cover your ears.

8. Once again notice any sensations, images, feeling and thoughts that arise in your awareness and stay in this hand position for a further twenty breaths.

9. Repeat the process above in the following positions:

   Neck – hands on collar bones
   Heart – hands on central chest
   Belly – hands on central abdomen
   Root – hands on pelvis

10. Having been through all of the hand positions, now allow the hands to be drawn intuitively to any place of need.

11. Spend as long as you wish attending to the body.

12. Return to wakefulness in your own way.

Record your experience in your Mindfulness Journal noting the perceptions that came to you in each of the hand positions.

If practising with others, take turns sharing your discoveries.

# 91 Offering Healing to Others

## What happens when people open their hearts? They get better.

HARUKI MURAKAMI

### Invitation

We are all born healers and we know the power of touch.

As a child, when you graze your leg you hold it or rub it better, parents instinctively place their hands on a distressed child, and a single touch for someone in need can remind them they are not alone.

Adding intention and visualisation to touch can make human contact even more healing.

### Mindful Tip

This practice leads on from the earlier ones in this section. You will find it useful to start with those before trying this one.

It is also possible to offer healing to someone who is not physically present. Use a teddy bear or a pillow to symbolise their body and go through the hand positions imagining them in front of you. You may find you even sense feedback as if you were working on them in person.

# PRACTICE 91

Ask the person receiving the healing (the Receiver) to lie down face up on the bed, massage table or a blanket on the floor. Sit or stand beside them and explain what you are going to do. Ask if it is OK to use touch during the healing and demonstrate the hand positions so they know what to expect. Invite the Receiver to close their eyes, relax and set an intention to receive the healing.

1. Rub the palms of your hands together quickly for about 30 seconds to commence the flow of energy. Imagine that your breath is connected to an infinite source of healing white light, infused with love, rejuvenation, joy and vitality.

2. As you breathe in, imagine the white light is filling your body and as you breathe out, imagine the white light is passing down your arms and out of the palms of your hands.

3. During each hand position keep this visualisation in mind, as it catalyses the flow of energy.

4. When placing your hands on the Receiver, use a cupped hand rather than a flat palm.

5. Begin by sitting or standing behind the Receiver's head and bringing your hands gently over their eyes. Do not press down but softly rest your cupped hands on their face with the centre of your palm above the eyes. No part of your hand should touch their eyelids.

6. Notice any sensations, images, feelings and thoughts that arise in your awareness and stay in this position for about twenty breaths.

7. When you sense intuitively that this hand position feels complete, move to the next by bringing your cupped palms to cover the Receiver's ears.

8. Once again notice any sensations, images, feelings and thoughts that arise in your awareness and stay in this position for about twenty breaths.

9. Repeat the process above for the following positions:

   Neck – hands on collar bones
   Heart – hands on chest (if male)
         hands off, floating above chest (if female)
   Belly – hands on central abdomen
   Root – hands off, floating above pelvis
   Knees – hands on knees
   Feet – hands either on or floating above as you wish

10. When the last position feels complete, listen deeply and allow the hands to be drawn intuitively to further positions.

11. Spend as long as you wish attending to further hand positions.

»

12. In bringing the practice to a close simply touch the Receiver on the shoulder and tell them gently that the healing is over. Give them time to gradually return from their experience and offer them a glass of water.

Ask the Receiver what they experienced during the practice and record their response in your Mindfulness Journal. Make notes of your own experience also.

# 92 The Body Scanner

## Doubt everything. Find your own light.

GAUTAMA BUDDHA

## Invitation

Despite the similar title, this practice is very unlike Practice 10, Body Scan. This exercise challenges your visualisation skills and offers a new way to experience the energy of self-healing.

## Mindful Tip

Create variations of this practice by changing the colour of the light in the body scanner. Note how each colour allows for a slightly different experience within the practice.

»

# PRACTICE 92

Begin by finding a comfortable posture and by bringing your attention to the breath. Take a few moments to let yourself arrive and allow the breath to draw you gently into internal awareness. Allow the gaze to soften, the eyes to close.

1. Take an inventory of how your body feels right now. Is there an ache, a pain, a sense of vitality, a tiredness, a heaviness, a lightness? Select three headlines that your body is broadcasting. Take five breaths here.

2. Now imagine standing a few steps in front of yourself.

3. Look back at yourself sitting down with your eyes closed.

4. There is a healing device in your hand. It is a silver tube about the length of a ruler. Holding it horizontally you see that it emits a brilliant blue light.

5. Intuitively you direct the light towards your own body that is still sitting in front of you. The light moves directly through your body and out the other side. You have never seen light behave like this before. Take five breaths here and watch.

6. Take the focus of your awareness now from watching the light moving through your body, to actually feeling it happening. Take five breaths here.

7. The light begins at the head. As it moves through, an incredible release occurs. Your mind feels like it is physically opening and clearing. The eyes relax. The airways clear. The breath deepens. Watch and notice. Take five breaths here.

8. The light moves to the chest, abdomen and arms. Let the light have its full affect and breathe deeply into it. Be your experience fully. Take five breaths here.

9. The light moves to the pelvis, legs and feet. Welcome the light and experience its brilliance within.

10. Before bringing the exercise to a close, take an inventory of how your body feels now.

    *What do you sense?*

11. Select three headlines that your body is broadcasting and notice what, if anything, has changed since the start of the practice.

12. Return to wakefulness in your own way.

Record your headlines from the start and end of the practice along with any other reflections in your Mindfulness Journal.

If practising with others, take turns sharing your discoveries.

# 93 Healing Tones

You have everything you need for complete peace and total happiness right now.

WAYNE W DYER

## Invitation

It is one of the little miracles of the Universe that every problem, issue, and poison has its own solution, resolution or antidote. These seemingly elusive gifts are often tucked away in a forgotten pocket, but they are still present and oh so close by.

This practice invites you to play with your voice and sounds to find some of the forgotten treasures you packed for your journey.

## Mindful Tip

Unless very confident with your voice you might feel more relaxed and free trying this one alone and out of earshot.

Remember too that your voice has infinite variations. Any time you need more of something in particular (wisdom, for example) you can adapt this meditation and go find it in your voice.

»

# PRACTICE 93

Begin by finding a comfortable posture and by bringing your attention to the breath. Take a few moments to let yourself arrive and allow the breath to draw you gently into internal awareness. Allow the gaze to soften, the eyes to close.

1. This exercise enables you to locate five different sounds that have a beneficial impact on the body.

   - *One to relax*
   - *One to clear the mind*
   - *One to open the heart*
   - *One to rejuvenate the physical body*
   - *One that connects to the frequency of love*

2. Start welcoming your voice by making the first sound that comes out of your mouth. It might be a rumble, a growl, a scream, a tone. Whatever it is: welcome it with open ears and see where it goes next.

3. Breathe in between sounds but continue the exploration allowing all and any sounds to tumble out.

4. Remember there is absolutely no attempt here to sound good or to sing in any recognisable way. Pure instinctive sounds work best for this practice so resist the urge to use words.

5. The first sound you are looking for is a sound that calms. Use your voice and your intuition to guide you into a hum, hiss, whistle, vibration or tone that feels relaxing to your body and mind.

6. Take as long as you need. You will know the sound when you find it.

7. Do not worry if the sounds do not seem beautiful or well formed. Sometimes a deep growling rumble is exactly what the body needs.

8. Once you have it, repeat it five times. Each time allow the body to fully resonate with the sound and experience its impact.

9. Now repeat the exercise for the remaining sounds.

10. Note that returning to this exercise may bring up new sounds for the same purpose. Allow this to happen fluidly. Nothing in the world of vibration is fixed.

11. Return to wakefulness in your own way.

Record your experience in your Mindfulness Journal seeing if you can describe each sound so carefully to enable you to find it more easily next time. Do remain open to the fact that the same sound may have a different effect at a later date and so you may have to find a new sound each time.

If practising with others, take turns sharing your discoveries.

# 94 Breath Medicine

Integrated meditation practice is like a healthy diet which is indispensable for maintaining your vitality and resistance to disease.

ALAN WALLACE

## Invitation

In this practice the breath is coupled with a specific intention in order to welcome a new experience into the body.

## Mindful Tip

You may find it useful to clarify your intention in writing so that it is specific and precise and ready to be applied within the practice.

»

# PRACTICE 94

Begin by finding a comfortable posture and by bringing your attention to the breath. Take a few moments to let yourself arrive and allow the breath to draw you gently into internal awareness. Allow the gaze to soften, the eyes to close.

1. Breathe deeply and acknowledge the breath as a powerful catalyst for healing.

2. Acknowledge your own ability to infuse the breath with intentionality, energy and purpose.

3. Listen to the body's call for healing. Note any sensations, images, feelings, words and thoughts that arise. Take five breaths here.

4. Now set an intention for this Breath Medicine exercise. Be absolutely specific and precise with your language; e.g.

   *My breath is infused with the energy of transformation.*

   Take five breaths here.

5. Hold the clarity of your intention confidently and courageously.

6. Allow the awareness to travel on the breath into the body, journeying to wherever it is needed.

7. Observe the breath as it transmits and delivers the intended frequencies. Feel them in your body.

8. Move back and forth on the breath until the process feels complete.

9. Return to wakefulness in your own way.

Record your experience of practising Breath Medicine in your Mindfulness Journal.

If practising with others, take turns sharing your discoveries.

# Advanced Visualisations

# 95 The Flowering Mind

## When I let go of what I am,
## I become what I might be.

LAO TZU

## Invitation

In any moment a flower is as open as it can be. If it were any more open, it would rip.

## Mindful Tip

To vary the practice, choose a different focus for the teaching within each petal. Variations might include:

*Vulnerability*
*Sadness*
*Pain*
*Letting go*
*Truth.*

# PRACTICE 95

Begin by finding a comfortable posture and by bringing your attention to the breath. Take a few moments to let yourself arrive and allow the breath to draw you gently into internal awareness. Allow the gaze to soften, the eyes to close.

1. Imagine your mind is a flower bud with five beautiful petals, almost ready to open. Observe it and notice this is the most beautiful flower bud you have ever seen. It is colourful, luminous and delightful. Take five breaths here.

2. One of the petals is beginning to open. Bring the full focus of your awareness to it now. Take five breaths here.

3. As the petal opens it unfolds with a teaching just for you about Stillness.

4. Allow the teaching to impact you first as a feeling. Take five breaths here, focusing on physical sensations.

5. Notice next if there are images, thoughts or words that accompany the feelings. Receive what comes with gratitude. Take five breaths here.

6. Repeat instructions 2–5 four more times with the following teachings behind each subsequent petal:

   - *Change*
   - *Love*
   - *Life*
   - *Joy*

7. Now contemplate the flower in its full glory with its five colourful petals. Breathe in full awareness of the wisdom in front of you.

8. Finally, allow the wisdom of the flower to sink down into your body. Notice the degree to which you are able to embrace the teachings.

9. Consider how you will move this wisdom into action in your life.

10. Conclude your practice in the energy of appreciation.

11. Return to wakefulness in your own way.

Record any teachings that were revealed in this practice in your Mindfulness Journal and reflect upon how you might take what you have learned into action.

If practising with others, take turns sharing your discoveries.

# 96 The Cave of Self-Realisation

Every man takes the limits of his own field of vision, for the limits of the world.

ARTHUR SCHOPENHAUER

## Invitation

Have you ever had a dream within a dream?

This practice explores a meditation within a meditation (within a meditation).

## Mindful Tip

No need to follow the instructions rigidly in this practice. Allow your mind to move freely through the ideas and simply observe what occurs within your awareness.

# PRACTICE 96

Begin by finding a comfortable posture and by bringing your attention to the breath. Take a few moments to let yourself arrive and allow the breath to draw you gently into internal awareness. Allow the gaze to soften, the eyes to close.

1. You find yourself looking down at the ocean following a path along a beautiful cliff. Feel the warm breeze against your face. The path is dotted with wild flowers, the sun is shining and the day is all yours. Take five breaths here.

2. As you walk down the path, listening to the waves crashing below, you notice a small vertical gap in the rocks. There is an occasional dart of intriguing blue light emerging from the opening. Take five breaths here.

3. As you peer in, you see a tunnel leading into the distance. Light is moving down the tunnel in an unusual way. Wisps and whirls of luminescence collect and dance along it. You follow, knowing that you are being invited to enter. Despite your initial caution, you feel safe and proceed.

4. Inside the tunnel the light leads you forward through a maze of passages. Your feet follow the twists and turns, your hands sometimes pushing against damp, cold rocks. Within a few moments you emerge into an enormous cavern. Take five breaths here.

5. The light now focuses your attention on a rock in the middle of the cavern. You see a vision of yourself sitting on this rock in meditation. Walking over, you take your seat. Closing your eyes, you fall into a deep state of meditation. Take five breaths here.

6. Within this meditation, you become aware of another gap in the enormous cavern. You walk over and notice that there is water trickling down; it sounds like there is a stream. Following along, the stream leads you to a deeper cavern filled with blue light. Your eyes adjust as they become accustomed to the blue dimly-lit cavern. Take five breaths here.

7. This cavern is filled with water, a huge underground lake. The blue light dances across the surface. In the middle of the lake is a rock. You see a vision of yourself sitting on this rock in meditation and swim across to take your seat. You fall into a profound state of stillness. Take five breaths here.

8. Within this meditation in the centre of the blue cavern, you become aware of a tunnel with colourful lights. Feeling adventurous you dance along the tunnel and emerge into an enormous chamber of spectacular colours. Take five breaths here.

»

9. The chamber is bejewelled with crystals on all sides. Crystals larger than you have ever seen. Bigger than you can believe. The energy of the light is nurturing in a way you do not understand. You feel loved, healed, made whole. You are totally surrounded by joyful waves of calm. Take five breaths here.

10. Unexpectedly, your awareness returns you to your meditation in the blue water cavern. You look around the hazy blue cavern taking a further five breaths here.

11. On your next breath your awareness returns to the first chamber that you entered. You notice you are still sitting on your rock in meditation.

12. As your eyes become accustomed to the light, you know it is time to return to the ocean path. You take five breaths preparing to return outside.

13. Retracing your steps through the maze of tunnels you find yourself once again with sunlight on your face and the sea breeze in your hair. You sit down on the warm grass and watch the ocean.

14. Here you sit taking as much time as needed to contemplate your inner journey.

15. Return to wakefulness in your own way.

Record your experience in your Mindfulness Journal.

If practising with others, take turns sharing your discoveries.

# 97 The Torus

Play is the only way the highest intelligence
of humankind can unfold.

JOSEPH CHILTON PEARCE

## Invitation

The torus is a donut-shaped energy vortex that can be
observed within atoms, cells, seeds, flowers, animals,
humans and galaxies.

Through the torus, the human body is linked to both
the micro and the macro, to nature, and to the Universe.

## Mindful Tip

Familiarise yourself with the shape and energy flow within
a torus by searching for images and videos online before
commencing this practice.

*Suggested Search Term: the universal pattern torus*

»

# PRACTICE 97

Begin by finding a comfortable posture and by bringing your attention to the breath. Take a few moments to let yourself arrive and allow the breath to draw you gently into internal awareness. Allow the gaze to soften, the eyes to close.

1. As you breathe, visualise yourself within a large torus.

2. Join your breath with the flow of energy circulating through the torus.

3. Focus on your heart. Take five breaths here. What do you notice?

4. What colours are present in the torus? Take five breaths here.

5. Recall a time in the last week when you felt afraid. Return fully to the experience. Take five breaths here and notice what happens to the torus.

6. Recall a time in the last week when you felt strong, supported or loved. Take five breaths here and notice how the torus responds.

7. Now, place your hands on your chest and breathe directly into your heart. What happens to the torus?

8. Explore and play until your practice feels complete.

9. Return to wakefulness in your own way.

Record your experience of playing with The Torus in your Mindfulness Journal.

If practising with others, take turns sharing your discoveries.

# 98 Meeting Yourself

Have good trust in yourself, not in the One that you think you should be, but in the One that you are.

TAIZAN MAEZUMI

## Invitation

How many times have you met yourself on the journey of life?

## Mindful Tip

This practice can also be done as a walking meditation in nature. Set out with the intention to meet yourself. Walk in quiet meditative awareness and allow your experience and the feedback you receive from the environment to lead you on.

»

# PRACTICE 98

Begin by finding a comfortable posture and by bringing your attention to the breath. Take a few moments to let yourself arrive and allow the breath to draw you gently into internal awareness. Allow the gaze to soften, the eyes to close.

1. Your journey begins in a little village in the countryside. Running through the pretty houses you notice a beautiful trickling stream.

2. Today is the day for a hike far into the forest beyond the stream. There is someone there to meet. Take five breaths here, in preparation for the journey ahead.

3. You set off early. The day is bright, the air fresh and warm.

4. As you move into the forest, the light changes. Soon surrounded by the sounds of crunching twigs, birdsong and windblown leaves, even the light seems to crackle and crease on the forest floor, and through the bracken.

5. Looking around, you notice a mist rising. Soon it is up to your knees. The mist leads you forward on your journey. Following, you take five breaths here.

6. There is a clearing ahead surrounded by a majestic circle of trees. It is so quiet and peaceful in the clearing that you decide to lie down and rest for a while. Take five breaths here.

7. Awaking from your rest you notice another figure sitting across the clearing. As the figure approaches you realise it is you.

8. The figure has a message for you. Listen carefully. Take five breaths here.

9. You sense you also have something to say to the figure.

10. Communicate your message now and listen for any response. Take five breaths here.

11. As time stretches out, you notice the mist drawing away from the clearing, and your time together is coming to an end.

12. Before leaving the figure and returning to the village, the figure offers you a gift to open at a later time.

13. Thank the figure, pack the gift in your bag and retrace your steps back home.

14. You will know when to open the gift.

15. Return to wakefulness in your own way.

Record your shared messages in your Mindfulness Journal and reflect upon your gift.

If practising with others, take turns sharing your discoveries.

# 99 The Pristine Singularity

True mindfulness is the awareness
that everything you encounter
is a vigorous expression
of the same living Universe as you.

BRAD WARNER

## Invitation

The Big Bang did not happen, it is *happening*.

In the very same way, you are *happening* now in this moment. It is this state of *happening* where experience and awareness merge that gives rise to The Pristine Singularity.

## Mindful Tip

If leading this practice for a group it is essential that you drop fully into the experience of this awareness yourself. The words will not be enough.

»

# PRACTICE 99

Begin by finding a comfortable posture and by bringing your attention to the breath. Take a few moments to let yourself arrive and allow the breath to draw you gently into internal awareness. Allow the gaze to soften, the eyes to close.

1. With each breath allow your perception of self, your story, your identity to fade into the background. Take five breaths here.

2. Let every single event, conversation, relationship and decision that has brought you to this moment disappear.

3. Move into direct experience of the now.

4. Allow experience and awareness to merge. Take five breaths here.

5. Experience and awareness merge further. Take five breaths here.

6. Here in The Pristine Singularity there is no doing, only being. Take five breaths here.

7. You and the Universe are alive as one. Take five breaths here.

8. The Pristine Singularity speaks. Take five breaths here and listen.

9. Ask yourself:

   *What does it feel like to be me in this moment?*

10. Next, call in all known and unknown aspects of self. Take five breaths here.

11. As your experience of self expands, meet it with the breath.

12. Notice the physical vibration of life now moving through on all levels.

13. Feel every cell teeming with abundance. Take five breaths here.

14. Contemplate the question:

    *Who am I?*

15. Stay with the question until your practice feels complete.

16. Return to wakefulness in your own way.

Note your experience of The Pristine Singularity in your Mindfulness Journal.

If practising with others, take turns sharing your discoveries.

# 100 The Open Doors

When one door closes another opens. Expect that new door to reveal even greater wonders and glories and surprises.

EILEEN CADDY

## Invitation

Within the inner world of awareness is a labyrinth of open doors.

## Mindful Tip

Once familiar with this meditation, you can ask the birds to take you anywhere within your imagination. Allow them to light the way and guide you.

»

# PRACTICE 100

Begin by finding a comfortable posture and by bringing your attention to the breath. Take a few moments to let yourself arrive and allow the breath to draw you gently into internal awareness. Allow the gaze to soften, the eyes to close.

1. Sit and breathe in gentle awareness. Notice where you are. Notice who you are.

2. There is a path to walk, a journey to follow and a unique contribution to make.

   *What will it be?*
   *How will you know?*

3. As you sit in contemplation, The Peacock appears with a majestic shake of his shimmering blue neck. Observe his gentle eyes and multi-coloured tail of glorious feathers. Take five breaths here.

4. The Peacock explains that he wants to take you to some places within awareness you have not been before. As he takes flight, to your delight, so do you. Take five breaths here.

5. Travelling together through the near darkness you can make out in the distance a labyrinth of tunnels encased in hazy white light. There seem to be travellers within them. There are also distant hubs where the tunnels meet and passengers connect, transfer, meet or move on.

6. Soon, the tunnels are left far behind and nothing familiar remains in this deep space.

7. Looking behind, you see a trail of light extending all the way back to the beginning. The Peacock explains that he weaves light through the Universe. Your mind cannot quite grasp this concept but looking around, you can see what he means.

8. As The Peacock slows he asks if you are ready to see one of your open doors. You silently answer. Take five breaths here.

9. The Open Door is ahead of you and The Peacock is giving you the choice to enter.

10. Your heart is beating in anticipation and readiness.

11. And then you are inside.

12. Time evaporates. All is clear. Take twenty breaths here as you are shown everything you need to see.

13. Explore fully and ask all of your questions. Take twenty breaths here and listen for the response.

14. When ready to contemplate your return, gather three words that will link you to this Open Door.

15. As you exit, you find The Peacock waiting to fly with you home.

16. Delight in the journey.

17. Delight in your return.

18. Return to wakefulness in your own
way.

In your Mindfulness Journal record
what you saw, felt and heard inside this
Open Door. Note also the three words
that link you back to this experience.

If practising with others, take turns
sharing your discoveries.

## In Closing

It has been an honour sharing my favourite mindfulness practices with you.
I wish you joy and happiness on your path of mindfulness.

*Forgive yourself often.*
*Keep coming back to your practice.*
*And, breathe.*

Thank you.

# Interview with the Author

### Why did you leave your career as a barrister to teach mindfulness?

The short answer is, because it felt right. I had practised law for almost a decade but I had been passionate about meditation, healing and human potential since I was a teenager. At a certain point, the call was so strong to create something new, that I could no longer ignore it. Although the transition was extremely hard, I am so grateful that my new work allows me to feel fully aligned in my life. I enjoy all the different ways in which I get to share mindfulness skills and love the freedom and challenge of running my own business.

### Where do you teach mindfulness?

I am based in London and offer 1–1 Mindfulness Tuition and Conscious Life Coaching to clients around the world. I teach weekend retreats periodically at Champneys Health Spa in the UK and occasional workshops in the US.

I also teach mindfulness to corporate clients. I set up *The Conscious Professional* in 2012 to provide wellbeing skills to overwhelmed professionals. I have been lucky to work with many forward-looking companies and find that there is a real desire amongst professionals to reconnect with their sense of equanimity, purpose and joy. My courses help them do just that. You can find out more at *theconsciousprofessional.com*.

### What inspired you to write a mindfulness book in this format?

Strangely enough I was leafing through a beautiful recipe book called *Genius Recipes* when inspiration struck. I thought to myself, wouldn't it be great if there was a book that described mindfulness skills in a really precise, easy-to-follow way. A book that you could leaf through and pick from, in the same way you might choose an exciting new dish for dinner. Initially, the book was going to be called *Genius Mindfulness Meditations*.

**The image on the book cover is bold and slightly mysterious. Where does it come from and why was it selected?**

The image is one of my own Fine Art Photographic works taken from a Soul Portrait of the aerial performer, Arian Levanael in 2013. I chose it because it felt calming, creative and inspiring and provided an eye-catching backdrop to the text. It was important to me that the book had the right design, energy and feel and the easiest way to achieve that was to incorporate my own art.

**Your Soul Portraits seem to capture something beyond the surface of the subject. How do you achieve that?**

My process seeks to witness subjects in the mindful space between stillness and movement. I have developed a technique combining healing, meditation, movement and digital photography. As I take a subject through the process they are invited to close their eyes and listen. I begin with gentle energy work and simple mindfulness practice. In time I invite the subject to interact with colourful fabrics. I pose questions and challenge them to answer only using the fabrics and movement. With eyes still closed, they begin to create by moving their body and the colours. When the time is right I pick up my camera and begin photographing. As the session evolves the questions move from the meaningless to the profound and as the subject drops deeper into playful expression, I am offered a glimpse beyond the surface, to the essence.

**Where can we see more of your art?**

My work is online at *soulportraitstudio.com* and I have fairly regular exhibitions in London and in the San Francisco Bay Area. My most recent show *Souls of Wisdom* was commissioned by Google and the Wisdom 2.0 Conference. It opened in Dublin, Ireland before travelling to San Francisco and then Oakland in California. My latest shoots were with Anna and Daria Halprin and I look forward to showing these new works soon. Upcoming exhibitions will be listed on the website.

**Other than meditation, how do you relax?**

I love to travel. My Dad was a commercial airline pilot and my Mum a stewardess, so I think it is in my blood! I love planning foreign adventures whether for work or pleasure and I have a big soft spot for tropical islands.

# References

**Practice 1**
Zen is a Japanese form of Buddhism that emphasises meditation and intuitive awareness as a path to enlightenment.

**Practice 2**
Thich Nhat Hanh is a Zen Buddhist monk, author and one of today's leading spiritual teachers.

**Practice 3**
Theodor Seuss Geisel (1904–1991) was an American writer and illustrator best known for authoring popular children's books under the pen name Dr. Seuss.

**Practice 4**
Dan Brule is a world-renowned pioneer in the field of Breathwork.

**Practice 5**
Rumi was a 13th Century Persian poet, theologian and Sufi mystic. His work transcends ethnic and national borders and is widely read to this day.

**Practice 6**
See 5.

**Practice 7**
William Shakespeare, *Twelfth Night*.

**Practice 8**
Mother Teresa (1910–1997) was a Roman Catholic religious sister and missionary who received the 1979 Nobel Peace Prize for her good works benefitting the sick and dying.

**Practice 9**
Kahlil Gibran, *The Prophet* (Wordsworth Editions, 1997).

**Practice 10**
Professor Mark Williams is Professor of Clinical Psychology and Wellcome Principal Research Fellow at Oxford University and the co-author with Danny Penman of *Mindfulness, A Practical Guide to Finding Peace in a Frantic World* (Piatkus, 2011).

**Practice 11**
Jack Kornfield is a bestselling American author and one of the key teachers to introduce Buddhist Mindfulness practice to the West.

**Practice 12**
Deepak Chopra is an Indian American author, teacher and alternative medicine advocate.

**Practice 13**
Anna Halprin is a dancer and choreographer credited as one of the originators of postmodern dance.

**Practice 14**
See 3.

**Practice 15**
See 13.

**Practice 16**
William James, *Life Mapping with Jesus: Finding Your Place in God's Eternal Plan* (WestBow Press, 2014)

**Practice 17**
Jack Kornfield, *The Art of Forgiveness, Loving Kindness And Peace* (Random House, 2010).

**Practice 18**
Sir Isaac Newton (1642–1726) was an English physicist and mathematician who is widely recognised as one of the most influential scientists of all time.

**Practice 19**
Marcus Aurelius, *Meditations of Marcus Aurelius* (Comelius H. Shaver, 1882).

**Practice 20**
Ram Dass is an American spiritual teacher and the author of the seminal book *Be Here Now* (Crown Publications, 1971).

**Practice 21**
Sogyal Rinpoche, *The Tibetan Book Of Living And Dying: A Spiritual Classic from One of the Foremost Interpreters of Tibetan Buddhism to the West* (Random House, 2012).

**Practice 22**
Louise Lynn Hay is an American motivational author and the founder of Hay House, she has

authored several self-help books including *You Can Heal Your Life* (Hay House, 1984).

**Practice 23**
Byron Katie, *A Friendly Universe: Sayings to Inspire and Challenge You* (Penguin, 2013).

**Practice 24**
Marianne Williamson is an American spiritual teacher, lecturer and author of eleven bestselling books including *A Return to Love* (Harper Collins, 1992).

**Practice 25**
Tom Ford is an American fashion designer and film director.

**Practice 26**
Thomas Moore, *Care of the Soul* (Piatkus, 1992).

**Practice 27**
Miuccia Prada is an Italian fashion designer and the businesswoman behind Prada and Miu Miu.

**Practice 28**
Eckhart Tolle was listed by Watkins Review 2011 as the most spiritually influential person in the World. He is best known as the author of *The Power of Now* (Yellow Kite, 2001) and *A New Earth* (Penguin, 2009).

**Practice 29**
Hans Christian Andersen (1805–1875) was a Danish author best remembered for his fairy tales such as *The Emperor's New Clothes* and *The Little Mermaid*.

**Practice 30**
Kahlil Gibran, *Treasury of Kahlil Gibran* (Open Road Media, 2011)

**Practice 31**
Alan Alexander Milne, *The Complete Tales of Winnie-the-Pooh*, (Dutton Children's Books, 1994)

**Practice 32**
Thich Nhat Hanh, *The Miracle of Mindfulness: An Introduction to the Practice of Meditation*, (Beacon Press, 1996)

**Practice 33**
Gautama Buddha, or simply the Buddha, was an ascetic and sage on whose teachings Buddhism was founded. He is believed to have lived and taught mostly in the eastern part of the Indian subcontinent sometime between the 6th and 4th centuries BC.

**Practice 34**
Nikola Tesla (1856–1943) was an inventor, electrical engineer and futurist best known for his contributions to the design of the modern alternating current electricity supply system.

**Practice 35**
Woody Allen is an American actor, comedian, filmmaker and playwright, whose career spans more than six decades.

**Practice 36**
Mahatma Gandhi (1869–1948) was the leader of the Indian independence movement in British-ruled India whose practice of nonviolent civil disobedience inspired movements for civil rights across the world.

**Practice 37**
See 36.

**Practice 38**
Gwen Costello, *Spiritual Gems from Mother Teresa* (Twenty-Third Publications, 2008)

**Practice 39**
Madeleine L'Engle (1918–2007) was an American writer best known for young-adult fiction, particularly *A Wrinkle in Time* (Farrar, Straus & Giroux, 1963).

**Practice 40**
See 28.

**Practice 41**
Unknown.

**Practice 42**
Lao Tzu was a philosopher best known as the author of the Tao Te Ching and the founder of philosophical Taoism. He is usually dated to the 6th century BC.

**Practice 43**
David Beckham is an English former professional footballer

who was named in the FIFA 100 list of the world's greatest living players in 2004.

**Practice 44**
See 28.

**Practice 45**
Herman Hesse, *Siddhartha* (New Directions, 1951).

**Practice 46**
Mary O'Malley and Eckhart Tolle, *The Gift of Our Compulsions: A Revolutionary Approach to Self-acceptance and Healing* (New World Library, 2004).

**Practice 47**
Carl Jung (1875-1961) was a Swiss psychiatrist and psychotherapist who founded analytical psychology.

**Practice 48**
See 33.

**Practice 49**
Helen Adams Keller (1880-1968) was an American author, political activist and lecturer.

**Practice 50**
See 19.

**Practice 51**
J K Rowling, *Harry Potter and the Half-Blood Prince* (Bloomsbury Publishing, 2014).

**Practice 52**
See 5.

**Practice 53**
Steve Maraboli is an author,

speaker and behavioural science academic.

**Practice 54**
Ursula K Leguin is an American author of novels, children's books and short stories, mainly in the genres of fantasy and science fiction.

**Practice 55**
The Dalai Lama is seen by Tibetan Buddhists as the Bodhisattva of Compassion and the patron saint of Tibet.

**Practice 56**
Unknown.

**Practice 57**
See 42.

**Practice 58**
Robert Frost, *The Road Not Taken, and Other Poems*, (Courier Corporation, 1993)

**Practice 59**
See 2.

**Practice 60**
Alice Munro, *The Moons of Jupiter* (Penguin Books, 1982).

**Practice 61**
Walt Disney (1901-1966) was an American animator, voice actor and film producer. He was a pioneer of the American animation industry and is best known for his cartoons such as Mickey Mouse.

**Practice 62**
Mitch Albom, *Have a Little Faith:*

*A True Story* (Hachette UK, 2011).

**Practice 63**
William Shakespeare, *The Tempest.*

**Practice 64**
Maya Angelou (1928-2014) was an American poet, memoirist and civil rights activist.

**Practice 65**
See 47.

**Practice 66**
See 13.

**Practice 67**
Albert Einstein (1879-1955) was a German-born theoretical physicist who developed the general theory of relativity, one of the two pillars of modern physics.

**Practice 68**
Ovid (43BC-18AD) was a Roman poet who lived during the reign of Augustus.

**Practice 69**
See 3.

**Practice 70**
See 64.

**Practice 71**
See 5.

**Practice 72**
Roger Ebert (1942-2013) was an American film critic, historian, journalist, screenwriter and author.

**Practice 73**
See 67.

**Practice 74**
Ralph Waldo Emerson (1803–1882) was an American essayist, lecturer and poet who led the Transcendentalist movement of the mid-19th century.

**Practice 75**
Henry David Thoreau (1817–1862) was an American author, poet, philosopher and historian.

**Practice 76**
Will Rogers (1879–1935) was an American cowboy, vaudeville performer, newspaper columnist, and stage and movie actor.

**Practice 77**
Charles M Schulz (1922–2000) was an American cartoonist best known for the comic strip *Peanuts*.

**Practice 78**
Jonathan Swift (1667–1745) was an Anglo-Irish essayist, poet and cleric best known for *Gulliver's Travels*.

**Practice 79**
See 13.

**Practice 80**
Cesar Milan is a Mexican-American self-taught dog behaviorist best known for his television series *Dog Whisperer*.

**Practice 81**
Confucius (551–479BC) was a Chinese teacher, editor, politician and philosopher.

**Practice 82**
Huang-Po was an influential Chinese master of Zen Buddhism during the Tang Dynasty.

**Practice 83**
Reshad Field (1934–2016) was an English mystic, author, spiritual teacher, and musician.

**Practice 84**
Georgina Eden is a healer and my current spiritual teacher. She is based in Vancouver and works with individuals and businesses guiding them from clarity into excellence.

**Practice 85**
Alan Watts (1915–1973) was a British philosopher, writer and speaker, best known as an interpreter of Eastern philosophy for a Western audience.

**Practice 86**
Leonardo da Vinci (1452–1519) was an Italian polymath widely considered to be one of the greatest painters of all time.

**Practice 87**
Mooji (1954– ) is a spiritual teacher originally from Jamaica.

**Practice 88**
Kahlil Gibran, *Mirrors of the Soul*. Translated by Joseph Sheban (Philosophical Library, 1965).

**Practice 89**
See 33.

**Practice 90**
See 5.

**Practice 91**
Haruki Murakami, *Norwegian Wood* (Random House, 2011)

**Practice 92**
See 33.

**Practice 93**
Wayne W Dyer (1940–2015) was an American philosopher, self-help author, and motivational speaker.

**Practice 94**
Allan Wallace, *The Attention Revolution: Unlocking the Power of the Focused Mind* (Wisdom Publications, 2006).

**Practice 95**
See 42.

**Practice 96**
Arthur Schopenhauer (1788–1860) was a German philosopher.

**Practice 97**
Joseph Chilton Pearce, *Magical Child* (Bantam Books, 1980).

**Practice 98**
Taizan Maezumi, *Appreciate Your Life: The Essence of Zen*

*Practice* (Shambhala
Publications, 2002).

**Practice 99**
Brad Warner, *Sit Down and Shut
Up: Punk Rock Commentaries
on Buddha, God, Truth, Sex,
Death & Dogen's Treasury of the
Right Dharma Eye* (New World
Library, 2007).

**Practice 100**
Eileen Caddy, *Opening Doors
Within: 365 Daily Meditations
from Findhorn* (Findhorn Press,
2007).

## Further Resources

*10 Mindfulness Meditations* by Neil Seligman is an audio album
of guided meditations to accompany this book.

If you have questions for the author about any of the practices, or
would like additional resources, please visit: **www.100meditations.com**

To book the author for Speaking Engagements, One-to-One Coaching,
Corporate Training Programs, or to sign up for Neil Seligman's monthly newsletter,
please visit: **www.theconsciousprofessional.com**

For more information regarding Neil Seligman's artwork, or to commission
a Soul Portrait Experience for yourself or as a gift for a loved one,
please visit: **www.soulportraitstudio.com**